FOUNDATIONS
FOR A THEORY
OF CONSUMER
BEHAVIOR

FOUNDATIONS FOR A THEORY OF CONSUMER BEHAVIOR

W. T. Tucker
UNIVERSITY OF TEXAS

HOLT, RINEHART AND WINSTON
New York · Chicago · San Francisco · Toronto · London

Preface

To anyone who knows the literature of marketing well, this book may be something of a puzzle. The form may be strange and the content even stranger. Therefore, it may be desirable to discuss the reasons for the peculiarities of the volume and explain its possible uses.

The title of the work, *Foundations for a Theory of Consumer Behavior,* is meant to be taken seriously. The two key words are *Foundations* and *Theory.* The first of these implies that there is no theory of consumer behavior, but that one is possible. And it states that the conditions such a theory must meet are adequately discussed within these pages. The second term is more difficult since it has been used somewhat loosely in marketing, just as it has in other business subjects. Anyone using it must explain how he uses it. In this volume the word "theory" refers to a statement that names the important factors in the system and gives the details of their interrelationship. An example may help.

Ballistic theory is concerned with the trajectory and point of impact of a body hurled through space. In general, both of these can be explained in terms of the original speed of the body, its weight, its shape and density, the nature of its movement, the angle of fire from the horizontal, wind direction, air density, and gravitational field. Any movement of the base from which the projectile is hurled is also important if one wishes to calculate forces required.

Ballistic theory is a theory because it deals with measurable factors, because it states their relationships in detail, and because any one factor can be fairly completely determined by a knowledge of all the others. Given all of the factors except the initial speed of the projectile, an engineer can determine what that speed was. Asked to change the point of impact, he can suggest several ways in which this can be accomplished—all of which will work.

It is common knowledge that the behavioral sciences are not as advanced as the physical sciences. What this means, in effect, is that no one has yet defined all of the factors in human behavior or determined the influence that each has on events. In fact, no one has really done a very good job of determining what an event is, that is, how to measure it or what to consider relevant about it.

Again, an example may help explain the dilemma. It is irrelevant to ballistic theory that John Gingrich is standing beside the 155mm rifle when it is fired. It may not be irrelevant that he is standing beside the person who selects a necktie. It is not relevant to ballistic theory that the gunner's father once carried an M-1. It may be relevant that the automobile purchaser's grandfather once owned a Ford.

Further, one may sensibly ask what consumer behavior is. When a man drives to work in the morning, is he engaged in consumer behavior? His car is using gasoline, which he must buy. He is wearing out the seat of his trousers. He is listening to a radio program on which there are occasional commercials. He passes a billboard advertising some product or service. He passes a car, which may be highly similar or completely unlike his. Is any of this consumer behavior? Is all of it? Has even a reasonable portion of consumer behavior been mentioned?

These are not trivial questions unless the entire subject of consumer behavior is trivial.

The format of this book is essentially simple. In the first chapter it attempts to discuss the ways in which the behavioral sciences relate to consumer behavior. And it attempts to assess the viewpoints, methodologies, and major constructs of these social sciences relevant to the problem of constructing a viable theory of consumer behavior. Obviously, the chapter is suggestive rather than exhaustive. It deals with a limited number of the basics of the social sciences rather than the fascinating details—many of which could fill a volume several times this large.

The chapter attempts to show why no one of the behavioral sciences is adequate as a model for consumer behavior by pointing out the ways in which each is applicable but limited.

The second portion of the book consists of descriptions of instances of consumer behavior. These cases are written by a number of people in order to secure a wide range of approaches to the subject. Since none of the authors is sure where consumer behavior begins or ends or knows what it includes, the cases are not parallel. One author may discuss the way in which Juan Navarro earns a living, another may contain information about what

Barbara was doing on the morning before she bought a maroon and white dress. It would have been simple for one person to have gathered this many cases. But if that had been done, the cases would have contained just those things that one person thought relevant to consumer behavior. Since most of the contributions were by persons who are not marketing specialists, but ones who have a variety of specialties, some of which are not even academic, it seems likely that much that might be overlooked by a single reporter is included.

If one reads the cases expecting to be told what consumer behavior is and how it works, he will be disappointed, perhaps bored. If he explores them to locate possible relationships or to determine the relevance of his own ideas on the subject, he will be rewarded. In fact, what he may appreciate most is a chance phrase or trivial remark that makes him realize the importance of some factor that he had not previously considered. Each of the cases is preceded by a brief introduction suggesting some of the things of interest in the case. The introduction does not *explain* the case or even interpret it. These things must await an adequate theory.

As every student of marketing knows, the literature is filled with lengthy discussion of ways in which businesses have studied the consumer, ways in which they have introduced new products to him, instances of involved advertising campaigns designed with his characteristics in mind, cases revolving around his presumed peculiarities as made clear through an analysis of snowball interviews or Likert scales.

Nowhere is there a single case of one consumer's behavior that starts before the purchase, analyzes the consumer and his circumstances, includes the purchase as an event, and then considers what happens after the purchase is made. Yet almost every basic text of the subject (and what must be a majority of all other books written about it) mention the fact that marketing is consumer-oriented or suggest that in some sense the "consumer is king."

In the absence of adequate consumer theory, it is not improper to consider with care the details of individual purchases by real people, to read their halting attempts to explain their own behavior, to attend the discussion of someone describing imperfectly the behavior of a friend or acquaintance.

The last chapter in the book was written after a perusal of the cases included here, and a number of others not included. It attempts to state where we are in the search for a theory of consumer behavior and to point the direction in which we must go to develop one that is satisfactory. It may be disappointing to anyone who thinks that marketing is on the verge of creating a full-blown theory of consumer behavior. Of course, the book ignores many bits and pieces of useful information about consumers in the interest of discovering an adequate over-view of the subject or a point of departure derived from the present state of knowledge.

The purposes of this book are several. First, it is designed to prevent the beginning marketing student from accepting uncritically the partial explanations of consumer behavior now available as final answers. Second, it is designed for those who have already discovered that there are no answers, and who wish to help in the search for useful questions. For anyone who uses it, it should open up avenues of thought while suggesting a reasonable firm base from which to proceed.

If the consumer is king, this might be regarded as his biography.

Austin, Texas   W. T. T.
September 1966

Contents

The
SEARCH for
RELEVANT THEORY

Consumer behavior is surely like other human behavior, subject to a host of influences that can be classified as social, psychological, environmental, physiological, economic, and the like. It can be regarded as a series of events in which the conditions of one time period are the primary determinants of the activities and conditions of the next time period. It can be conceived as a goal sequence in which an apparent goal becomes a stepping stone to some further goal, each chosen in turn because it represents the greatest of pleasures or the least of pains. There is no great intellectual effort involved in imagining causal effects that flow backward from the future, forward from the past, inward from the surrounding world, or outward from some deep organic process.

In effect, consumer behavior is the principal a priori of business. It precedes executive decision making and all the activities of business. At the same time consumer behavior is the only justification for business: a hot dog is to eat, a road is to drive upon, and a motion picture is to watch.

There is a strong tendency on the part of students of business and business men to study consumers *en masse* and their behavior in truncated segments. The result is that innumerable statements can be made about brand preference for coffee in Colorado, or TV-viewing habits in Philadelphia, or traffic patterns at Fourth and Main. Obviously such information about consumers is valuable if one is engaged in making instant coffee, buying TV spot-commercial time or planning the location of a retail store. In fact, modern business efficiency is just as dependent upon consumer information as it is upon a developing technology; and greater efficiency

1

clearly demands improved consumer analysis as well as technological change.

It is usual to regard the failure of an Edsel or a gourmet-food line as a loss for the Ford Motor Company or General Foods only. Yet even the most casual analysis points out that the loss is a common one suffered by the entire economy. When vast productive and distributive resources are committed to a product people do not want, or do not want in sufficient quantity, the loss is society's.

There is a common interest, then, in our understanding of consumer behavior that is as broad and as deep as our interest in economic growth or the so-called standard of living. Perhaps it is even somewhat broader. The getting and spending of the world, the very operation of the economic machinery, not only provides the stuff of living—it places its own imprint on the character of human life. Most American children learn the value system of the supermarket before they can spell their own names or recite the Lord's prayer. While the work week may have been shrinking, it seems probable that the shopping week has been expanding, if one includes the hours spent in gathering, or merely attending to, information about the market; the upward trend in time devoted to the spending portions of economic activity must be quite sharp.

An improved understanding of consumer behavior seems to have two useful consequences: first, it should find application in the search for increased economic efficiency; second, it should provide some of the information needed to evaluate the noneconomic influences of a system.

Current Knowledge about Consumer Behavior

Current knowledge about consumer behavior is fragmented. Neither the social critic who complains about TV commercials or the poor quality of modern toys nor the business executive who plans a new product has a reasonably cohesive theory within which to arrange the bits and pieces of information he possesses. That means that the gathering of information about consumers is considerably less systematic than it might be. Most research efforts are related to particular package designs or particular advertisements or particular products. The results, therefore, are not additive. A company may learn which of two packages is preferred by the largest number of consumers and yet not discover what qualities make for an acceptable package.[1]

---

[1] Over the last decade work of increasing theoretical interest has appeared as a real revolution developed in that portion of the academic community devoted to the study of business subjects. There is, for instance, a rapidly growing literature on brand loyalty in which sophisticated theoretical positions are discussed in the light of imaginative empirical research.

There is a strong temptation to suggest that some potential theory of human behavior would be as applicable for business in its dealing with consumers as vector analysis is for engineers in designing a bridge. Almost certainly no such careful and exact calculation as that of the engineer is possible in predicting human behavior. But that is not to say that some impenetrable barrier to improved prediction lies exactly at the frontiers of existing knowledge. The quasi-sciences of human behavior are really less than one hundred years old and already they have provided conceptual tools of great value—despite the obvious theoretical turmoil that characterizes the disciplines themselves.

The social sciences are the most obvious source from which to borrow theory. Concepts derived from them should not be merely analogous to some portions of consumer behavior but identical, or nearly so. In some cases such identity exists. Personality, if it is a categorical variable and can be measured, must be as important in consumer choices as in other choices. Status, to the degree that it is understood, can hardly influence the choice of mates but not the choice of mattresses, the nature of one's relationships to people but not one's relationship to things. To say this is not to say that consumer theory must absorb all the concepts or stated relationships of the social sciences. Nor does it suggest that there are not other known relationships and concepts from the biological, physical, or natural sciences that may not be more appropriate. The social sciences themselves have borrowed. And it is important to recognize the source of their theory. If they conceive the human in terms of a thermodynamic system, it becomes necessary to ask whether this is an appropriate analogy.

The frequent use of the notion of cognitive dissonance in discussions of consumer behavior, for instance, demands more than the recognition of cognitive dissonance as a circumstance relating to the simultaneous existence of conflicting notions within the organism.[2] This dissonance is said to be motivating in that it encourages behavior designed to reduce the dissonance. If one fails to realize that this is essentially a homeostatic theory, based on the concept of an "ideal" state (quite comparable in fact to psychological concepts dealing with thirst or hunger, but derived from more basic biological processes) one is ill-equipped to understand its insufficiency or the nature of cases it fails to explain, and may, in fact, overlook powerful notions such as rationalization or even fail to see the relationship between the two.

Many of the analytic techniques and constructs of the social sciences

---

[2] For the past few years students of marketing and marketers have used cognitive dissonance to explain a wide variety of events in their day-to-day conversation if not their literature. The term comes from the experimental work Leon Festinger carried out in the 1950s. *See* Leon Festinger, *A Theory of Cognitive Dissonance*. New York: Harper and Row, 1957.

have been applied to the study of consumer behavior. More of this borrowing has probably been from psychology than from other areas because of that discipline's attention to the manipulation or apparent control of subjects whether these be rats in a maze or patients on the psychoanalyst's couch. The stimulus-response framework of experimental psychology has clearly suggested that if one can provide appropriate stimuli, the probability of desired reactions can be maximized. And most studies of consumers have been directed toward the encouragement of particular reactions such as the purchase of a package of chewing gum.

Psychological Models

The basic psychological model is highly rationalized. It presumes a dynamic psycho-physical system that is continually moving out of balance, as the level of sugar in the bloodstream decreases and increases. The internal drive state (in this case hunger) pushes the individual with a strength related to the degree of imbalance. The discomfort or tension of imbalance causes the individual to seek a suitable response (in this case eating food), and the reduction of the discomfort or tension is pleasurable and acts to reinforce the same response (eating) when the drive state again increases to an effective level.

Subject to a host of primitive drives like hunger and secondary drives that are built upon the primaries in fairly direct fashion, the individual slowly learns what responses are successful reducers of what sorts of tensions. The apparently random behavior of the newborn infant becomes purposive and goal-oriented under selective reinforcement. On the simplest level, he learns to scratch where it itches.

The mature individual is, in effect, a biological mechanism utilizing a complex set of habit patterns, all of which are related directly or indirectly to some hedonic consequences described as pleasure seeking, pain avoidance, drive reduction, or the like.

The basic concept may be simple, but it is capable of seemingly endless elaboration and refinement. And, it provides a frame to which the particulars of behavior can be attached readily.

A few examples should suffice to demonstrate the elaboration and attachment. A person smells a steak broiling and suddenly announces that he is hungry. Analysis: perception of the internal state is not continuous and automatic. At low levels the internal state can be completely ignored. A dam level or threshold applies. No water spills over a 70-foot dam whether the water level behind it is 2 feet or 68 feet; only when it reaches some critical level can it be sensed from below as the first few drops spill over. But in sensation and perception there is also variability in dam level. The external stimulus of the steak smell sensitizes the individual to hunger levels not normally felt, or, conversely, external stimuli may lower the threshold to internal stimuli such as the hunger sensation, bringing them into awareness. It is important here to recognize that the broiling steak aroma can only elicit hunger in the individual who has previously eaten steak (or something like it) and had that behavior reinforced. The association of steaks and the particular aroma of steaks allows one of these to serve as a sign for the other. Of course, no two broiling steaks smell exactly alike. The actual particles of matter suspended in air cannot be of both the same kind and concentration whenever someone broils a steak. How then can one associate the unique odor of *this* steak broiling (accompanied by all of the other odors in the air) with other slightly different odor combinations that must have been present when one previously had steak? Psychologists accept stimulus generalization as the solution to this theoretical problem. Identity is clearly not required in a variable world. One must be able to recognize the color green without having seen *exactly* this shade of green before, or traffic lights would prove nonfunctional.

External stimuli cause responses that serve as internal stimuli in still further S-R connections, suggesting rather complex chains of stimulus-response sequences. The fact that one thing like a smell can have at least some of the response-eliciting character of another, like a steak, is clearly required in the system. And the possibility of sensory inputs that are not consciously attended to is at least implied, since levels of steak odor that one cannot recognize may still elicit the sensation of hunger.[3]

Of course, there is no single behavioral frame that will begin to suggest the subtle, and often critical, distinctions between the numerous psychological theories. But it seems fair to claim that most have as critical features the external stimulus, the internal state, the behavior itself that often requires an object, and some affective reaction that makes the behavior more likely to recur or less likely.

A somewhat closer look at each of these features and their relationships seems desirable. First, the external stimuli seem relatively simple. They are, of course, merely the physical constituents of the world—the noises, pressures, temperatures, sights, smells, and tastes that surround us if one wishes to suggest them in sensory term. The most obvious character these stimuli have is that they do not stimulate different people in the same way or even the same person in identical ways at all times. In fact, some persons can taste, hear or see things that others cannot. At a somewhat

---

[3] During the mid-1950s there was a brief flurry of excitement over the possibility that advertising messages that were delivered so rapidly that the individual was not conscious of them could influence his behavior in a direct and powerful way.

more complex level the very stimulus that is followed by an instantaneous sensation of hunger in one individual may lead to marked nausea in a second. Almost everyone has heard of the slaughterhouse employee who drinks blood or knows that some persons regard the head as the most delicious part of a herring. And almost everyone has heard some variant of the story of the man who eats a delicious new food in a foreign land only to vomit on being told what it contained.

Stimuli can be categorized in terms of the sensations or responses they elicit or in terms of some independent measuring device, such as a thermometer or light meter. The entire rhetoric of Aristotle is, in effect, nothing but a description of complex stimuli stated in terms of probable response. The same holds, of course, for music theory, such artistic techniques as linear and aerial perspective, or choreography. That there is no comprehensive nor accurate dictionary of stimuli suggests the complex and variable character of sensation or perception, which may seem intuitively to be the simplest elements of behavior theory.

Analysis of the internal state has never seemed quite as direct or obvious as has that of stimuli. Of course drives could be measured objectively in terms of the liquid level of the body, the sugar level of blood, or various chemical imbalances.[4] Or they could be approximated by stating the relative length of deprivation: two days without food, six hours without water. And they could be categorized in terms of the goal object or behavior that would reduce them. Lists of drives have been so developed. Primary drives like hunger, thirst, and sex are obvious. Less basic drives or needs such as those for affection, prestige, or safety seem legitimate if somewhat less obvious. But in the end the result of attempted categorizing has become almost tolerable chaos. One who takes Occam's razor seriously can reduce all apparently different human drives to one, such as sex, power, or survival. And anyone who wants to emphasize the diversity of behavior ends up by positing such complex secondary drives as that for the welfare of loved ones. The desire for novelty ultimately explains *all* behavioral variation when it sets out to explain a few specific difficulties. And the need for exercise provides a satisfactory motive for all of the apparently nonpurpose activities that any careful observer is forced to note.

On the one hand, the notion of drives and motivation makes considerable sense and proves useful. On the other, it seems unnecessarily fanciful to posit a death wish in order to explain why people bite their fingernails.

Currently, the subject of motivation is in turmoil. Apparently a major reason for this turmoil is the physical analogy on which the basic notion of motivation is based. An object does not move unless some force is

---

[4] The terms "drive" and "drive state" are used here in a nontechnical sense in order to avoid a number of rather difficult and unresolved questions.

applied. The movement of balls on a pool table can be explained in terms of amounts and direction of physical energy and some measure of friction. Balls move only when struck by the cue or another ball. By analogy, it is presumed that human actions are all in response to sufficient and appropriate motivation. But it is clear that human motives are not all highly directive. True, hunger seems to lead to certain appropriate actions that assuage hunger and are more or less common to the species. But it is fairly clear that eating can be used similarly as a process to assuage anxiety, loneliness, or boredom—crudely described drive states or tensions that may be thought of as driving toward action without driving toward any particular behavior or class of behavior. The simplest such apparent ambiguity lies in the drive state variously described as anger, fear, or of the sort that is said to prepare the organism for "fight or flight." Anxiety is an almost completely nondirective drive state that seems to have as its most obvious characteristic a sort of anti-instrumental quality. The more anxiety one has over the possibility of making a particular blunder, the more likely it is to occur.

While a great deal has been discovered about the nature of basic drives and their influence on behavior (particularly animal behavior), discussions of human motivation are often most fruitful when they focus on goal objects and the responsive activities carried out in connection with them without much consideration of the central nervous or other processes that might be analogous to a primitive drive state. The response processes themselves are the operational aspects of personality and have the advantage of being overt and measurable. It is not unlikely that one might learn more about the reasons for the purchase of an automobile by examining the car itself and watching how the owner drives and cares for it than by studying any of the stimuli or internal states that preceded the purchase.

Particularly interesting is the discovery that response patterns may become functionally autonomous so that they are elicited by a broad range of stimuli, for some of which they may be relatively inappropriate. Almost everyone knows people for whom aggressiveness or avoidance are common responses to a host of varying situations. Functionally autonomous responses of this sort often lack the practical relevance of hunger-eating analogy that is the basis for much of psychological theory.

The pool-table analogy of motivation might make better sense if one were to imagine it covered with bells, pieces of glass, lumps of tar, and so forth as well as balls. When the cue ball strikes the glass, it breaks. When it strikes the bell, it rings. And when it hits the tar, the result will depend in large measure upon the temperature of the room.

There is little question but that some reactive process tends to make particular behavior more likely or less likely to recur. The simplest classic statement is that pleasure stamps in; pain stamps out. It is a remarkably solid generalization, as six-word generalizations go. But it simply doesn't cover all situations, nor is it possible to state the nature of pain and pleasure with enough precision for scientific purposes. Modern psychology is well aware that it is dangerous to view human behavior in a cause-and-effect framework combined with the analogies of Newtonian physics. One might suggest that while students of the subject are clearly seeking causal relationships in human behavior, they are also involved in the search for a richer, subtler, or more satisfying meaning for the word "cause."

Probably no study of human behavior has been so evaluatively neutral as the psychological. One does not, in the psychological view, discuss whether a TV commercial is "worth" viewing; one simply assumes that if it is viewed, it is (in the only meaningful sense) worth viewing. Such objectivity is too often missing in the discourse about consumer behavior. On the other hand, one may question whether a system in which the character and quality of human life can only be spoken of in terms of tensions, imbalances, and reinforcement is sufficiently rich for the purpose of all behavioral analysis. The problem is not simply one of misunderstanding the difference between an art and a science.

The Economic Model

The primary economic model relevant to consumer behavior is as explicit but not so complex as the psychological. It adds few important constructs save those that make the essentially direct hedonic position somewhat more operational. It does stress an aspect of choice behavior that psychology generally pays little attention to: the scarcity of resources. The decision not to buy or not to save may be a concomitant of the resource level more than the drive level. Economists tend to disregard the drive level, except in such fairly crude terms as Keynes' propensity to spend, just as psychologists tend to treat resource levels as given.

There are suggestions in economic analysis that one *may* forgo an intense pleasure in order to—and here words fail. Almost anything that can be said suggests a greater desire of some sort simply because of English syntax and Anglo-Saxon predisposition. The closest approximation is to suggest that one does not choose what one wants so much as what one can choose. This statement does limited but important violence to the notion. In formal analysis economists accept the distortion in order to deal rigorously with choices in terms of assortments of choices.

Imagine a child at an amusement park. He has limited time; he has limited money; and he has a limited capacity for sensation. He might well take a fairly unexciting ride first, not because it offered the greatest return for his expenditure in any usual sense, but largely because it would not seriously deplete his ability to derive thrills from subsequent activities. In any case, his scarce resources might be more important in the process of choosing than any combination of drive states, stimuli, or reinforcement. Of course, this is not to say that choice behavior of any sort defies purely psychological explanation, even if one deals with only that restricted portion of psychological theory suggested earlier.

Economic theory is, in the analysis of consumer behavior (or consumer demand), as elegant as in other areas of analysis. With a limited number of assumptions it concludes that there is one, and only one, assortment of rides and exhibits in the amusement park that will maximize the child's satisfaction. The normal presumption is that the consumer knows the price and availability of all alternatives and can properly assess the satisfaction to be derived from each. Such an assumption is surely less acceptable for the child than for an adult, surely less valid in an amusement park than in the supermarket. It has a certain intuitive acceptability in either case.

The second assumption is that sequential rides on the carousel will each deliver less satisfaction than the last. This is the notion of marginal utility so thoroughly developed by Marshall. Other assumptions state possible relationship of the carousel to the roller coaster. The child may prefer the roller coaster to the carousel, the carousel to the roller coaster, or he may have no preference between the two. And his preferences are transitive. If he prefers the carousel to the roller coaster and the roller coaster to the fun house, he must prefer the carousel to the fun house.

Given these assumptions it is possible to develop mathematically precise descriptions of the ways in which the child's choices of assortment will change when prices or any of the rides change or when he is given more money to spend. And, if one could measure the utiles (unites of satisfaction) involved in the various rides, he could predict the specific assortment that would be chosen. But even lacking this, he could, by observing the assortment actually chosen, draw some conclusions about the shape of the child's indifference curve. An indifference curve is one connecting all assortments that deliver equal satisfaction, for instance:

$$5 \text{ Carousel} + 3 \text{ Roller Coaster} = 10 \text{ C} + 1 \text{ RC} = 3 \text{ C} + 8 \text{ RC}$$

The one chosen will be whichever of these combinations (or of the other possible equal-utility assortments that lie on the curve) costs the least. When the cost of the roller-coaster ride is low compared with the cost of the carousel, the assortment chosen will be quite different from that chosen when the cost of the roller-coaster ride is high in comparison to that of the carousel.

The methodology of a discipline is seldom neutral. Experimental psychology, from which the tightest and most hardheaded theoretical constructs derive, has simply not dealt with techniques that encouraged the study of what might be referred to as "economizing" in this sense. The closest approximation to the notion may be Zipf's principle of least effort, which is only roughly comparable.[5]

While it is a gross oversimplification to suggest that there is a single economic model, virtually all that concern consumers explicitly have at their heart the concepts of maximizing satisfactions, marginal utility, and limited substitutivity. And it is largely on the basis of such concepts that its relationship to an emerging theory of consumer behavior rests.

Economic theory is far from sterile. But much of its relevance is implicit rather than explicit, and the work of digging out the implicit insights of the major economists has hardly begun. It has been difficult, in fact, to study the full implications of their major theses.

The Socioanthropological Model

The essential characteristic of the socioanthropological model is that it explains all behavior (and, in effect, judges it) on the basis of what can be called social location. This might be described by the dictum: If you were he, you would do as he does. Sociology and anthropology are not mutually uncontentious. But they are sister disciplines in a sense that sociology and psychology or economics and sociology are not. That is, they share a viewpoint, a considerable amount of methodology, and much the same basic set of assumptions. Sociology has contributed both the most explicit and elaborate theory. Anthropology has supplied a wealth of detail, primarily on primitive cultures, suggesting the great variation in human organization and activity for which social theory must account. That many of the sociological concepts have the range and application to find use when one discusses either the Hottentot or the corporate chief is sufficient reason to regard them as major concepts in the analysis of any human behavior.

Both presuppose a biological organism, as does psychology. And it is generally granted by all of these social sciences that human behavior is in part a function of the sinews, nervous system, and organs bequeathed the individual.

The focus of social study is on the variables that seem to be associated with particular sorts of behavior. The simplest of these (and perhaps the least well understood) are sex and age. The two-year-old male is not and does not behave like a two-year-old female. Nor does a two-year-old male

---

[5] George K. Zipf, *Human Behavior and the Principle of Least Effort*. Reading, Mass.: Addison-Wesley, 1949.

behave like a five-year-old male. Actions suitable for the sex and age are impressed upon the individual in numerous subtle ways and at unbelievably early ages so that it becomes impossible to distinguish clearly between the natural or intrinsic distinctions of age and sex and the social requirements that relate to age and sex. The Italian children who begged and pandered among the American soldiers of World War II were in many ways older than their benefactors. It would be fairly simple (assuming the validity of anthropological findings) to train a small society in which men cried freely and women were stoic.

In any case the female is led to accept feminine activities and roles while the male is bent in other directions. A progressive, changing set of expectancies discourages fixation at any particular set of behavioral patterns. The child who is encouraged in cutely destructive behavior today may be chastised severely for it tomorrow when he has grown "too old for that kind of thing." The male of advanced age must learn that he is no longer to play the dominant role in affairs expected of him even a few years previously.

Variations in age behavior can often be explained by position in the family. The youngest child in the family is notoriously slow in putting aside babyish ways, while the eldest may be drawn toward maturity in action before his time. Similarly, differences in life-cycle stage are related to behavioral changes that cannot be completely understood on the basis of age and sex alone. The twenty-two-year-old female who is single has different interests and activities than one who is married; and the young mother of the same age is another variant.

The primacy of these concepts has been demonstrated time and again in sociological and anthropological studies that cross racial, cultural, and class boundaries. The slow maturation rate in man, the relative incapacities of the young and the aged, the character of human reproduction: all clearly limit the forms of family life and the possible social roles available to the individual. Since membership in some family group characterizes normal human experience, relatively broad typologies are possible. While psychology implies that common stimuli and common internal states will lead to certain similarities in human behavior, such as the drinking of water, it suggests few additional limits to the development of individuality beyond those related to the physical character of stimuli and physiological possibilities of the human body. In other words, the psychological model seems to be most applicable to behavior that is common to all men or that is highly individual. In contrast, the socioanthropological model tends to concentrate on the behavioral differences among certain categories or types and describes the modal character of each type.

Of course, typology is a characteristic of all systems of knowledge. At its most successful it is capable of generating theoretically invaluable tools such as Mendeleef's table of elements or descriptively cogent systems such as that by which the zoologist classifies life forms.

So far as human typology is concerned, no truly adequate system has been developed. The ancient classification of individuals into phlegmatic, choleric, sanguine, and bilious types was not really much less successful than the introvert, extrovert categories popularly discussed in the 1930s or the inner-directed, other-directed, autonomous types popularized in the 1950s. Most psychological typology has been based on some sort of continous variable extremely difficult to measure. Intelligence, aggression, paranoia, endomorphism, and rigidity suggest something of the rich and varied way in which psychology has approached the development of a typology. Sociology and anthropology have used continuous variables such as age, but have also made considerable use of discrete variables such as sex or motherhood. Relatively easy to measure or determine, the fundamental classification system of these two closely related social sciences are probably the most successful attempts at a human typology that is directed toward the prediction or understanding of behavior.

The attempt to characterize individuals by stating their relations to others clearly does not have to cease with the family group, since there are a host of other groups, institutions and the like, which exert influences not unlike those of the family. The total sum of these might be said to describe the individual's social location. The assumption is that social location largely determines behavior, or at least explains most of the variation in behavior.[6]

While it is impossible to mention all of the various criteria that have been used to describe social location, a number are so relevant to any such description that they deserve discussion.

The face-to-face relationships found in small groups that are often together are generally regarded as more consequential than less frequent or less intimate relations. One's family, friends, close neighbors, work and play groups can almost be thought of as establishing the effective social parameters of the individual's world. He can be described largely in terms of his relationship to these groups, which exert immediate control over his behavior. Of course, such control is seldom overt. The individual both anticipates with considerable accuracy the reactions of these groups to his behavior, and evaluates behavior himself in virtually identical terms. The

---

[6] If one wishes to think in a cause-and-effect framework, it should be pointed out that the assumptions that underlie this viewpoint seem to be as follows: individual behavior is largely the consequence of present interaction with other people and things and of previous interactions of that sort. Social location is merely a means of suggesting the nature of those interactions.

result is that more often than not the very actions that please him the most are ones the relevant groups evaluate highly.

The tendency to emphasize the importance of relatively intimate group relationships is partially a function of the ease with which such things can be studied and the frequency with which they have been studied. Most anthropological studies are, in fact, of relatively small familial or tribal groups, which have few major external social connections. Since all studies must end at some point, the more distant the relations, the less likely they are to be included in research programs. Yet the young executive may move from California to Ohio on the decision of someone in New York whom he has never seen, while his wife and children protest; and the dock worker in New Orleans may walk off the job because of a strike vote taken by the Baltimore local; the IBM salesman may wear garters because of a dictum laid down thousands of miles away by a man long dead; the customer in Atlanta may patronize a particular store because of an exclusive dealership negotiated in Chicago.

There need be no argument about whether the small, intimate groups focused on by the folksy tradition in sociology or the major institutions and organizations of modern life influence behavior more. Either can be a critical variable. Membership in the United States Army, General Electric, or the Republican party can often explain behavior that is otherwise inconsistent with social theory. But pressures and influences from an intimate, face-to-face group can support defiance of the full powers of government.

Obviously, social theory is best applied to modal behavior rather than unique events such as the emergence of a Faulkner or the assassination of a president, although like most systems of knowledge it has supporters who will essay anything.

Between the impersonal dicta of an establishment and the warm influence of an intimate lies a host of other influences that stem from membership in ethnic or racial groups (which are not groups in the strict sense), from religious or political affiliations, from loyalty to labor or occupational associations, from the impersonal intimacies of an Ann Landers or Marlboro man. The social location of an individual can be stated in terms of a few relationships, if one is satisfied with relatively crude stereotyping; a complete locational statement can be made of no one. At present there are no explicit theories suggesting where one should stop in considering social connections or how one can determine the relevance of those included or excluded in an analysis.

But there are at least two major thematic sources from which the groups, individuals, and institutions derive the values, and role anticipations, and behavioral modes they encourage or discourage. The first of these is historic and is normally referred to as culture. The second relates to existing major social divisions and is usually called class. The two are not discrete, nor are they comprehensive unless one defines them in the broadest possible sense.

Culture is an inference from the observable continuity in behavior of reasonably broad collections of people. It explains such minutiae as shaking hands or rising when a woman enters the room as well as such general values as belief in democratic political forms or respect for aggressive physical action. And it differentiates social roles as well as describing common behavior patterns. The 2300-year-old oath that defines the medical doctor's responsibilities starts: "I swear by Apollo the physician, by Aesculapius, by Hygeia, Panacea and all the gods and goddesses. . . ." The religious reference and the later mention of slaves has no present social relevance, suggesting the nature of cultural change. Some passages such as the promise to keep secret the arts of medicine except to appropriate initiates are generally disregarded by a profession that requires the broad dissemination of information. Others, such as the physician's duty not to divulge of his patient that "which ought not to be spoken abroad," are upheld by contemporary courts as well as medical associations.

Of course cultures are never completely stable; apparently something analogous to entropy in the physical sciences or forgetting in the individual is constantly in operation. But the major sources of cultural change seem to be cultural mixing or environmental changes of various sorts. A Norman conquest or the immigration of Italians into New England leads to the inclusion of words like "beef" in the English language or pizzerias in Massachusetts. The Industrial Revolution in effect predicted labor organizations, and the development of the automobile entailed changes in courting behavior, but only because supporting cultural values and precedents were available.

A knowledge of the cultural streams that are embodied in the groups with which the individual interacts does much to explain the behavioral possibilities open to him and his own emotional reaction to the choices he makes.

To some extent the social class to which a person belongs is a screening device that limits his cultural heritage. Beyond this it tells a great deal about how he fits into the contemporary, social dynamic. He may dream of existence as Horatius at the bridge, Davy Crockett or Batman, but he follows his destiny to the steel mill or the bean fields or the chemical laboratory and behaves as though these were his goals within the context of social class.

Social class is less clear and less restrictive in the modern world than it was in the recent past; and it is of less influence in some lands than others. But it remains a more important determinant of human behavior than the members of an "open" society always choose to admit. The plight of the American Negro can be largely stated in terms of low social class and limited cultural heritage, neither of which can be put aside rapidly. If one includes the cultural attitudes of other elements of society, the case becomes complete. Only the fact that other social conclaves of similar class and culture cannot be readily identified makes the Negro's chance of rising in society seem as small as it does. Nor are the assaults on his human dignity uniquely different from those experienced by social climbers in general, although others may be better able to camouflage their origins and thus avoid discrimination.

Goals and aspirations, which virtually define a number of aspects of behavior, are largely class determined. Manners of dress, preference in furniture styles, even drinking habits tend to move along class lines. Studies of sources of advice and counsel suggest that information generally moves horizontally in society and that the desire to be like the members of a superior or inferior class is relatively unusual, however much one may believe he wants the prerogatives of that class.

The middle-class male may dream of being a beachcomber with as much effect as the lower-class male who may dream of sudden wealth. Neither is likely to have the emotional commitment to make the dream a viable goal; The fact that some do is inadequate evidence that most can or desire to.

It is common knowledge that education is the most usual course for upward mobility. But the process is quite probably misunderstood. The subject matter generally taught in schools may be largely irrelevant. The presence of a middle-class foster mother in the form of the second-grade teacher, replete with the values and attitudes of her class is surely a more important variable. Public education merely ensures that most students will have the opportunity to see the middle class in action for a rather large number of hours each year and be weaned away from any other class to which they belong. The presence of middle-class instructors in all of the classrooms of a nation, in private schools, public institutions, colleges, and universities undoubtedly has led not only to upward mobility among the lower classes but to fixity in the middle class itself and probably to effective downward mobility in the highest classes. It is quite possible that an aristocracy can maintain its uniqueness only with teachers who are individual servants or slaves and that the closest approximation possible in an institutionalized school system is the development of a sort of upper middle-class snobbery.

But by its very nature the school is most effective with the classes near the middle of the social spectrum, and in a century or so it can hardly be expected to have homogenized a nation. Class realities remain useful variables in the prediction of behavior.

The most obvious relationship between the psychological and the sociological models lies in the areas of goal objects and reinforcement. First, the goal objects appropriate to any of the wants are culturally and socially defined. The Maine lobster is not an appropriate object for hunger in Israel despite the possibility of air-freight shipment. For the industrial salesman the large and unusual order is probably comparable to a scalp for the Indian brave of the last century.

Second, social approval is a sort of generalized reward that is appropriate for any behavior. In essence, it is functionally universal in much the way that certain behavior patterns become functionally autonomous. Nowhere is this clearer than in the small child who holds up its hurt finger to be kissed. Social approval may actually be a reducer of all drives, even including the ones such as hunger or thirst that it cannot satisfy physiologically. The story of the Spartan boy with the fox gnawing at his gut has numerous parallels in hunger strikes, public suicides by fire, and perhaps even the behavior of injured athletes who fail to realize how badly they are hurt until they reach the locker room.

However, stating the variables of one discipline in the terminology of another is quite different from creating a single model that subsumes both conceptual systems. Obviously, an adequate theory of consumer behavior will have to accomplish that task.

Other Models

There are many other models or theoretical concepts that seem potentially useful in the construction of a theory of consumer behavior. One of the most appealing of these is homeostasis, the process by which the blood stream keeps tending to move into balance. The most obviously homeostatic process involves cooling and warming operations that make it possible to say that the normal blood temperature is 98.6 degrees. Highly similar processes tend to maintain certain red corpuscle counts, blood sugar levels, and the like although not with such remarkably precise control.

Homeostasis seems to state reasonably well the total consuming and purchasing processes of the individual family, with inputs of food, clothing, furniture, TV-picture tubes, and the like, relating to some norm for the home. For instance, one can readily imagine the home in which the male head's stock of white shirts tends toward eleven. That is, when fewer shirts are available, purchases are likely. These purchases should tend to be larger, the further the stock is below eleven or the more rapidly it is presumed that existing shirts will have to be discarded. And one could suggest "normal" levels for other goods either in terms of individual items such as salt or in terms of classes of merchandise such as food.

The homeostatic model has several obvious failings. The first might be explained in terms of a simple growth function. It is obvious that the situation of a hunter, fisherman, or stamp collector may be one of greater wants. Two fishing rods or three rifles or a thousand stamps can indicate the desire for more in an almost systematic way, as the tree needs more water, the larger it grows. It may even be that such growth in wants is essentially exponential, held in check only by economic realities.

A second problem lies in the difference in the "normal" levels of merchandise and the difference in kinds of merchandise that characterize different families and individuals. Social theory can moderate the apparent shortcomings here by suggesting that there are large classes of individuals for whom homeostatic definitions of normality can be made, and one can point in analogy to the different normal blood temperatures of the different species. And, since all animals are not characterized by homeostasis in blood temperature, it might not seem outrageous to imagine that the notion applies as a model for consumer behavior only in certain social classes or cultures and that the real problem is one of defining the conditions under which homeostasis applies. The evidence on social change makes it clear, of course, that efforts to examine consumer behavior in such a way would be at best of small and temporary value.

Lastly the concept of homeostasis is wildly inappropriate to situations in which the interests of the individual undergo change. Probably more stamp collectors start modestly, grow enthusiastic, and then lose interest completely than continue to experience continually growing demands. Typically such persons tend to pick up new interests that may be as completely different as drag racing or ceramics. The growth model is perhaps appropriate to explain the demise of interest in a particular hobby or even a vocational pursuit, if one wants to deal with a platonism of traits or interest, each possessing its own life cycle or its own required inputs for survival. But the parallel is not persuasive and it begs the question of new interests, their origin and development.

Perhaps the best theoretical analogies lie in the learning and "forgetting" analysis of experimental psychology, despite the fact that it does not pretend to deal with more than a limited number of the possibly relevant factors—powerful as these may be in laboratory situations where other variables are either controlled or unconsidered. A possible alternative lies in genetics. If one takes social contacts to be "like" sexual relations in some sense, and if one grants that "the child is father of the man," the relevance of genetic theory becomes clear. The individual at "time one" is essentially a product of the individual at "time zero" combined with whatever dominant and recessive traits (in terms of cultural rather than genetic material) he has had social intercourse with during the interim. The notion is particularly pleasing since it allows one to speak somewhat realistically of the cultural or social sterility of the British, who seem to resist change of any sort, with the relative fecundity of the American, who may on limited social interaction "take up" almost anything from water skiing to Zen. Change in an individual may, then, be in some ways comparable to change in a species, with mutation serving as a counterpart to the unusual and seemingly unexplainable change while cultural, class, or other interactions (like genetic combinations) describe the usual directions variations in behavior take.

Recent discussions of decision making and problem solving seem to have direct application to consumer behavior, although the concepts involved are not inherently different from those of the basic psychological model mentioned earlier. The particular contributions of decision theory lie in the formal evaluation of alternatives and the sophisticated way in which uncertainty of outcome can be handled. There is no complete agreement on the elements of the process, but the following list is a reasonable approximation of current points of view.

The *goal* or *objectives* of the individual or group involved form the context for decision-making analysis. They state the terms in which evaluation must be carried out and sometimes the magnitude. In the classic melodrama that turns on the foreclosure of a mortgage the objective is stated in terms of dollars, and a critical number of dollars is involved.

Alternatives state the possible courses of action. These are normally characterized by relative uncertainty of outcome. But the cost of choosing a particular alternative is usually conceived as known. A retailer may know that he can purchase a particular appliance for $125, but he is not certain whether he can sell it for $150, $225, or $120.

Prediction systems, which can be extremely complex, are used to determine what the possible outcomes of each alternative are and how likely each outcome of each alternative is. Such prediction systems have been constructed with great precision for games of chance such as roulette. And these, in effect, serve as the model for prediction systems in general.

Evaluation of the alternatives is now a mere matter of calculation. For example, imagine an owner of a piece of property who has a standing offer of $30,000 for the property. He believes that there is a reasonably good chance that it may be purchased by a major oil company. His realtor tells him that such a sale should bring $50,000 for the property but that there is only about a 25-percent chance that such a deal can be worked out. A new purchaser shows up and offers $38,000 for the property on a forty-eight hour take-it-or-leave-it basis. What should the owner do? If the above statement is accepted as the most accurate analysis of the situation, the evaluation is as shown in Table 1.

Table 1

AN ESTIMATE OF THE VALUE OF DIFFERENT ACTIONS

Alternatives	Possible Outcomes		Probability of Outcomes		Evaluation
Sell Now	$38,000		1.00		$38,000
Hold for Sale	$50,000	×	.25	$12,500	
	$30,000	×	.75	$22,500	
				$35,000	$35,000

It is fairly obvious that the decision in this case can be made quite readily if a reasonably precise statement of goals or objectives is available.

The example is a simple one that includes no conversion of present dollars and future dollars to a common base. And the situation itself has been manipulated to allow only a limited number of possibilities and to make calculation fairly easy.

There is some similarity between consumer decisions and decisions of the sort suggested here. A consumer must evelute articles in order to choose among dresses or hats or houses or cars. In fact, there must be some mechanism by which he decides whether to purchase a camera or a refrigerator that is not completely unlike the conversion of the satisfaction to be derived from either into common dollar terms.

It should be recognized that the decision model is quite similar to certain aspects of both economic and psychological theory. But the frequency with which a point of view recurs has little to do with its adaptability to additional areas of thought.

The Use of Models

Model shopping is an interesting process. Much of the progress in human thought seems to have been based on the knowledge of certain relations and the perception that these are in some way analogous to another situation. The discovery of such analogues is both valuable and stimulating, perhaps comparable to the location by a writer of an apt simile or metaphor. And the ultimate in such endeavor is undoubtedly the location of a mathematical model that will state the relationships under examination well enough so that one can stimulate them and predict outcomes in the world of events by manipulating the model.

The obviousness of this in mid-twentieth century may make us a bit impatient with new fields of study. And, rather than attempting to understand the matter in its full, ripe reality, we may make hasty assumptions about the character of the world and develop quantitative statements that approximate our own relative ignorance of affairs. Such attempts are splendid when one remembers and admits all of the simplifying assumptions. It may be somewhat more usual to try to explain them away. In scholarly work "hoist by his own petard," translates into "trapped by his own analogy."

This volume is not designed to create a working model or even to suggest the simpler sort of apt analogy. It is designed rather to accomplish three things. First, in this chapter it has suggested that there are many sources of theory relevant to a study of consumer behavior. Both the biological and behavioral sciences are literally spilling over with well-formulated and conceptually exciting theories that cannot be ignored by the student of consumer behavior, even if he does not accept their full relevance to his own subject matter. Beyond this they are studded with bits and pieces that they have not themselves assimilated. It is common knowledge that the physical sciences and mathematics are similarly loaded.

Second, the bulk of the book is devoted to examples of consumer behavior, developed and written in the way some reporter thought most revealing. While many of the contributors had special disciplines of their own in the social or behavioral sciences, each was asked to view the affairs he reported in whatever way he felt did them the most justice. The notion was that reports would vary in emphasis and intention and that a careful perusal of them would at least suggest what consumer behavior is, what its major elements are, and how one may best view it.

Third, the last chapter, written after reading and rereading the cases submitted, attempts to determine where we are in our pursuit of a theory of consumer behavior, to recommend an overview that seems appropriate, and to suggest the next steps of the chase.

The following pages are devoted largely to the raw data a theory of consumer behavior must explain.

1 / Introduction to
A FAMILY PURCHASE

Peter Rigby, age eight, has outgrown his baby furniture. For two years he has collected advertisements of early American maple furniture like that of a nursery-school friend. With the purchase of Christmas presents impending, his family finally turns its attention to furniture for Peter and his younger brother, and purchases it from a country discount store in a nearby town.

There are several ways in which to report events. One of these is to determine what explanatory factors are important and then to shape the material to construct a practical demonstration of the ways in which the factors operate. Another is to attempt as accurate a reporting of events as possible without trying to demonstrate the relevance of a particular viewpoint. "A Family Purchase," like most of the cases contained in this volume, follows the second course.

In effect, such a report says to the reader: "You discover the relevant elements and make the generalizations." It is an approach that is particularly appropriate when a subject has not been thoroughly investigated and when there is little experimental evidence relating particular variables to particular processes. To anyone who wants nothing but predigested ideas, a case of this sort can be quite annoying because it has much of the formless rambling and repetition of everyday life, which does not interpret itself. To the individual who wishes to try out his ideas or to discover new ones, the very lack of a conceptual structure is exciting. He has the opportunity of discovering the questions to ask and considering possible answers implicit in the individual case. Further, he can attempt to test these against his own knowledge, and other cases in order to determine whether his notions relate to general characteristics of consumer behavior or merely specific situations.

While there are a number of interesting aspects of this case, such as the interaction of family members in the process of making a decision and the question of social influence from outside sources, it might be well to concentrate for the moment on two less obvious implications contained in the account.

21

The first area concerns consumer information and the relative difficulty involved in getting it. The family starts on its quest without satisfactory knowledge about brands, stores, or prices. Peter, an eight-year-old boy, starts the search and continues one aspect of it. In fact, for a two-year period he is the only individual in the family attempting to provide any of the information needed. (In the process, he puts some pressure on the other members of the family to consider the matter and apparently succeeds in establishing the general character of the furniture to be sought.) Later, the father seems to be the principal investigator, making decisions about when other members of the family should be brought into the process. The suggestion is that informational constraints play an important part in establishing the context for decisions and that the nature of the search explains the character of those constraints. A failure to discuss the matter with friends would have eliminated any possible purchase from the discount retailers. A failure to visit the local store would have made price comparisons difficult.

How should a theory of consumer behavior treat the matter of information and the search for information? It could simply be considered as given and then disregarded. Or it could be thought of as a major aspect of the process deserving a complete theoretical substructure of its own. If the latter seems appropriate, it becomes necessary to determine the ways in which information, sources of information, and investigative processes can be defined and distinguished usefully.

A second matter of some importance relates to the timing of the purchase. The writer suggests that the purchase could appropriately have been made as much as two years earlier, and there is little doubt that it could have been delayed further. A peculiar set of events seem to have triggered the beginnings of a serious search. These include the Rigby's habit of shopping early for Christmas, the family attitudes toward toys as presents, and Peter's attitudes toward clothes as presents. In this case the triggering mechanisms are not clearly related to the level of need or desire. Is it possible to think of desires as having levels of intensity with three sub-ranges? The first of these is of such low level that no action will be taken, the second is a level where action is possible but depends upon some external force being brought to bear on the situation, the third being a level in which the press or demand alone pushes toward action. Or does it make more sense to think of levels of desire as lying along some simple, undifferentiated continuum?

It should be pointed out that the case was not selected to pose these questions. The questions were induced by a reading of the case. The material from which many other relevant questions can be inferred is contained here. It seems unnecessary to focus attention on what are probably only a few of the aspects of consumer behavior and by indicating that these are somehow the "right" aspects to consider.

The approach of this volume is to emphasize that the question of relevance to consumer theory is an open one in which discussion and exploration are not only appropriate, but necessary.

Of course, cases of consumer behavior can be related to a variety of managerial situations. The original interest in Peter Rigby's furniture was stimulated, at least in part, by magazine advertisements of "Paul Revere" furniture which was stocked by the local "Gamma" store. The store was in fact visited, but the sale was made of a different brand and in a store many miles away.

Two rather major policy questions are implicitly raised. First, what changes in terms of pricing, advertising, selling, product differentiation, or other elements of the marketing mix would have been required to complete the sale of "Paul Revere" furniture to the Rigbys in the "Gamma" store? Both manufacturer and retailer operations are concerned. Second, are there enough customers like the Rigbys to make such changes in the marketing mix more profitable for either the manufacturer or retailer or both?

A FAMILY PURCHASE

Paul H. Rigby, *Director, Center for Research, College of Business Administration, Pennsylvania State University*

The purchase to be described resulted from a family decision and a remarkably unanimous one. Although each member influenced the decision and felt rather strongly about some aspect of the purchase, there was general satisfaction with the outcome. The purchase to be described resulted in the acquisition of new bedroom furniture for our two sons, Peter, age eight, and Mark, age six.

Early Roots of the Purchase

The roots of the purchase began to form when Peter was five years old. At that time both boys had in their respective bedrooms the original baby furniture with the exception of the beds. Both were sleeping in adult-size

Hollywood beds. For a table Peter was still using his infant feeding table that we had repainted. A chair had come with the table. His clothes, some toys, and those priceless treasures of boyhood—pebbles, strings, worn-out batteries, and so forth—were kept in an unfinished dresser that we bought and painted to match his repainted table. Other toys were placed on a set of homemade shelves. Mark found himself with a somewhat better dresser that had been purchased prior to Peter's birth by one of the grandmothers who was contributing to the nursery furnishings. Mark also had a toy box and a set of homemade shelves. He had two very small chairs and a little table built for preschool children.

When Peter was five we enrolled him in a nearby nursery school. Because his birthday falls in December, he was not quite old enough to go to public kindergarten but was too old to stay home and wander about the house. The school was a fairly popular one in our neighborhood so a car pool was organized to take five children to the school. In this car pool was a little boy named Paul Newman with whom Peter became very friendly. In fact, Paul became his best friend and the two played together as often as possible.

In Paul's bedroom there was a set of maple furniture, which most people would classify as *Early American*. It was a very well known national brand (to be called here Paul Revere), which carefully designs the various items so that they will fit together and give the effect of built-in furniture. Typically, one will find advertisements showing furnished rooms where dressers, bookshelves, cabinets, and desks are arranged along two or three walls creating the built-in effect. The furniture is ideally suited to economize on space.

Peter was most impressed with Paul Newman's furniture and decided that he would like to have his room furnished the same way. During the next two years Peter regularly noted advertisements in magazines of Early American maple furniture and particularly bedroom furniture by Paul Revere. When allowed, he used to cut the advertisements from the magazines and add them to his store of treasures.

It is a little difficult to determine exactly why Peter became so attached to Early American maple furniture, and particularly the Paul Revere type. Undoubtedly, the presence of the furniture in his best friend's bedroom was a significant factor especially when compared with what he had in his room. Peter is a very energetic and enthusiastic person who is always anxious to explore and try new experiences. He is an outgoing person who readily interacts with children and adults whom he has just met. It is not unreasonable to assume, therefore, that a person with this type of personality will react to his environment and to the behavior and tastes of others. Furthermore, his expression of interest in this Early American furniture did not meet with any disapproval at home but on the contrary with some approval. He was allowed to cut out the advertisements and probably even heard statements indicating approval of this type of furniture if not the brand itself.

The Decision to Buy Bedroom Furniture

Last summer when both boys had reached the ages of five and seven (they would be turning six and eight the following fall and winter) their mother, Dotty, and I began to discuss the need to purchase some new bedroom furniture. Obviously they had more than outgrown the furniture which they were using with the exception of the beds and possibly, the dressers. The little tables were much too small for them. Furthermore, Peter did not have any room to put the many models he was now building. We were also beginning to think about Christmas gifts. We had, in the past, purchased a number of gifts for the boys as well as other members of the family well before Christmas. One year we had more than three-quarters of our Christmas shopping completed by the end of August. This year we were particularly concerned with our Christmas shopping because we had moved the previous fall to Columbia, Missouri from Houston, Texas, and found that local shopping facilities were severely limited compared with Houston. We were planning on making a trip to New York later in the summer and were considering the possibility of doing some of our Christmas shopping there.

As we discussed Christmas we also raised some question about continuing the emphasis in the boys' Christmas gifts on just toys. We felt that possibly the time had come to buy them something other than just toys but yet also buy them something they would enjoy receiving. Clothes were, of course, an obvious possibility but Peter on other occasions had raised some objections to clothes as gifts for birthdays and Christmas. As we talked we hit upon the idea of buying the boys some bedroom furniture for Christmas; this would give them something they needed, something they wanted, and something other than just toys.

Shopping Begins

Now that we had decided to buy the furniture, we faced the questions of what kind of furniture, how much to get, how much to spend, and where to get it. When we were married, we purchased virtually all modern furniture for the house. Over the years our taste in furniture began shifting and on occasion we had discussed what other types of furniture we would like if we were to buy more. We had a rather mixed, or more appropriately, nondescript group of furniture in the family room. We began to lean toward the idea of furnishing the family room in Early American. We had already purchased a maple rocker for Mark's bedroom but after Mark was a year old, we had moved it into the family room. We thought that if we were to buy the boys some new furniture we could take Mark's dresser and refinish it in maple or something darker and use it to begin the furnishing of a combination guest room and study. We thought we would place one of the boys' Hollywood beds in the guest room as well. Dotty had indicated some interest in French Provincial for our bedroom. I did not lean too strongly in that direction, preferring Early American if we must shift from modern.

The general setting was, therefore, rather conducive to Early American furniture for the boys' room. Peter had already developed a firm preference on the matter and we were generally in favor with the idea. Mark, who was a little young when Peter began to form his attitudes toward bedroom furniture had begun to express an interest in Early American. Mark is not as aggressive or outgoing as Peter. He also tends to be influenced by his older brother, which to a great extent explains his choice of Early American.

The choice of furniture on the part of the various members of the family happily coincided and there was no need for a family council to resolve the difference. If there had been a serious difference some device would probably have been used to secure the boys' peaceful acquiescence, if not support, for something other than their original choice.

We decided that we would like to get the Paul Revere-type of maple furniture, which is designed to fit together in a somewhat modular fashion. One can buy this type of furniture in various combinations of cabinets, tables, desks, bookshelves, hutches, and beds. Dotty liked it because it has a built-in effect, and also creates a very orderly impression—something often difficult to achieve in a boy's room. We also liked the colors, since we both favor darker-tone woods. This type of furniture is also very economical in space. We concluded that this would be very desirable for the boys' bedroom now that they shared a room and later when they would have separate rooms. We were living in a rented house, which was smaller than the one we had had in Houston but were planning to move into another house so the boys could have separate rooms again. When they were again in separate rooms, we could add furniture and still maintain the general decor.

Making the Purchase

The particular brand of furniture which first came to mind was Paul Revere, the furniture which Peter had seen in Paul Newman's room. It was a nationally advertised brand and well known. After moving to Columbia we also began receiving advertisements from a local furniture dealer who specialized in Early American furniture and carried Paul Revere. Every so often we received a notice indicating certain types of Paul Revere were on sale noting that the price of the various items of Paul Revere tended to be rather high even when on sale.

Because the price was high we did not go directly to this store (the Gamma Store) to look at their furniture. First we considered buying from one of the other furniture dealers in town. I visited all of the local furniture stores in town, excepting the Gamma Store, and asked to see their bedroom furniture for boys. I did not ask specifically for maple or Early American. Nothing I saw proved to be very interesting. I saw some oak and some maple but was unimpressed with the appearance and the price. The general availability of this type of furniture and many other desirable items was quite limited.

We were generally unhappy with the variety and selection available in Columbia. We also missed the department store sales and the discount houses of Houston. As we discussed this general discontent with friends we learned of a rather interesting retailing phenomena in mid-Missouri. We discovered that there were retailers in some of the Missouri towns who specialized in the regional selling of a particular class of items at a very low price. The practice was to sell the class of items at something approximating discount house prices and to offer free delivery and maintenance service in the region. In one town for example, a retailer handled a wide variety of nationally advertised electrical appliances, selling them at a very good price and giving the customary installation and delivery service at no price increase even though the customer might live in a town 40 or 50 miles away. We heard of many such operations and even of one which sold automobiles this way.

Upon hearing of this retailing pattern we inquired to learn if there were any furniture dealers who operated in this fashion and were told that there were two located within 100 miles of Columbia. We were told that both carried nationally advertised furniture that they would deliver free and that their prices were quite good. We were warned, however, that sometimes there were rather long waits for the furniture to be delivered— as long as six weeks.

We decided that we would investigate these two retailers, but before doing so would check in Columbia with the Gamma Store to get a good look at Paul Revere. We wanted to have some specific information on price and quality that we could use to compare with whatever furniture we found in the two stores we were about to visit in the towns of Alpha and Beta. We found the Gamma Store and the personnel to be very pleasant. It was rather crowded but neatly arranged. We were shown the Paul Revere, and it was very attractive and substantial. The prices, as we expected, were somewhat above what we were interested in paying. We then drove on to the store in Alpha.

The Alpha store was a fairly large one and had a wide variety of furniture. We asked to see their furniture for boys' bedrooms. We were shown some maple and oak. The price was considerably below that asked for Paul Revere but so was the quality. The maple finish was a veneer and the inside of the drawers were poorly finished. Furthermore, the drawers did not fit tightly. Since we were not looking for oak we did not look at it too closely although it seemed to be better built than the maple. Dotty also objected to the approach of the sales personnel. They quoted us what they indicated was their standard price but then said that they would let us have a discount. The discounted price was well below Paul Revere. Dotty felt that there was a falseness in the sales personnel's approach, which first suggested a standard price and then offered a discount implying that we were receiving some sort of special consideration. From what we already knew, we concluded that the discount was the standard price. Just before we left, the sales clerk indicated that the store did carry a type of maple furniture to be referred to here as Early Williamsburg. They did not, however, have any samples in stock and so we left the Alpha Store somewhat discouraged, but drove on to the town of Beta still hoping to buy some good quality furniture at a good price.

After arriving in Beta, we had considerable trouble finding the Beta Store. We finally located it with the help of a local filling station attendant. We asked him where *The* furniture store was located and he immediately knew what we wanted. We drove up in front of the Beta Store but were not convinced we had located our quarry. There was no sign. We drove around the block a few times and finally decided we had indeed found the store. We parked and walked in to find ourselves in what appeared to be something of a warehouse. It turned out not to be quite a warehouse but there were certainly no efforts to display furniture as is done in the usual furniture store or as did the Alpha Store. There were people who seemed to be wandering about rather aimlessly and we could spot no sales personnel.

We commenced to wander about and finally located some Early American bedroom furniture. We found a greater variety than we had seen at the Alpha Store. Where we could find prices they seemed to be very good ones. At last someone came to wait on us, and we discussed some of the furniture that we had seen. We also inquired about prices. The sales person was quite straightforward and quoted a standard price on everything we inquired about without any mention of discounts. The prices were quite comparable to the so-called discount prices at the Alpha Store and of course, below the prices of the Gamma Store. We were also pleased with the quality of the furniture that we saw. We found some maple that was very attractive and turned out to be the brand, Early Williamsburg, which the Alpha Store said they carried but did not have in stock at the time. We also saw some dark oak that we liked. We collected information on prices for both the dark oak and the maple. The sales clerk told us that the store would deliver free to our house on one of their delivery trucks that apparently made two to three trips a week to Columbia. While at the Beta Store, we also discovered that people in St. Louis on occasion go there to purchase their furniture.

Both boys exhibited considerable interest in looking at the furniture but their interest in looking at furniture began to wane the longer we stood around waiting for a clerk to talk with us. Because of the store's very casual approach, there is no concern in providing prompt service. There were not enough clerks and people were allowed to wander about as typically happens in any discount store. As we compared the oak and the maple, the boys did make it clear they preferred the maple. We pointed out some of the advantages of the oak but they were unconvinced. Toward the end of our visit as we were waiting for the clerk to give us some final information on the maple, both boys became very restless and anxious to be on their way. The only way we could assuage their restlessness was to point out that it was their furniture that we were buying. I have the impression that the boys had more or less reached the point that they had made their preference clear and therefore there was really little need to stand around waiting and looking—"Order the furniture and let's go home."

We drove home with our information and proceeded to consider what would be the best. In spite of our original orientation toward the Early American maple we were now thinking about the oak. The oak was dark, which removed one of the objectionable aspects of oak. It was also very sturdy, which we thought would be a good idea since the furniture was to be used by two growing boys. After some consideration we decided, however, to stick with the maple. The prices were virtually the same and both boys were firmly convinced that they wanted maple. Mark was particularly adamant about wanting maple.

In Columbia we talked with several people who had purchased furniture from the Beta Store and the reports were all good. We were also told that they made no service charge on credit sales. We decided, therefore, to buy the furniture from the Beta Store and to buy Early Williamsburg. We liked the furniture, it was pretty and well built, and a nationally known brand. This last point was most important since the store itself was such a casual operation we had no other real basis upon which to rely for the quality of the furniture.

We proceeded to make up our order for a set of bunk beds, two commodes, two desks with chairs and a hutch to go on top of one of the commodes. With our order we asked if the merchandise could be delivered before Christmas and what credit terms could be extended. We waited some time to hear from the Beta Store and after a while began to wonder if we would hear from them at all. We decided one morning to call them and learned that the furniture was being delivered that day and that they wanted us to pay one-third down and the rest in ten equal monthly payments with no service charge. Later that morning the furniture did arrive. It came in crates and we had it stored in the back of our basement. No receipt was requested and no bill was delivered. In fact, we never did receive a bill or invoice through the mail. The only paperwork involved was our checks sent to them. It became very obvious that the Beta Store conducted business in a most casual, informal manner. This apparently allowed them to reduce their overhead. We couldn't help wondering, however, about their credit losses.

The boys were at school when the furniture was delivered, so I was able to hide it in the back of the basement behind various and sundry items. Our plan was to unpack the furniture Christmas Eve and place it in the living room where we would have the Christmas tree.

We had various plans for the furniture that was now in the boys' room. The mattress from the Hollywood beds would go on the bunk beds. The box springs would be stored in the basement with the thought that one day one of them would be placed in the combination study and guest room, an item in our future house. Mark's dresser would be refinished in maple or something darker and also placed in the guest room. The little tables and chairs would go to the basement and be placed in the children's play area. I would acquire Peter's dresser to add to my workshop area where I needed a place for supplies, tools, and so forth.

On Christmas Eve we unpacked the furniture and found most things in good order with two exceptions. Instead of sending us drawer-type commodes they sent cabinet types. One of the chairs they sent was slightly cracked. We debated over the commodes and decided that actually they would prove more satisfactory for the boys' clothes than the drawer type since they did have small drawers at the top and the desks had a great deal of drawer space. Christmas day we put up the bunk beds and had considerable trouble. Finally we got them up but felt that we did not have the correct parts. The day after Christmas we called the Beta Store and they apologized for not having explained that bunk beds can be set up in two ways, one of which allows for a guard rail and ladder. We wanted the latter and they agreed to send the needed parts plus another chair. (Incidentally, no other store had explained the option on bunk beds.)

In two or three days the delivery truck arrived with the new parts for the bunk bed but the wrong chair to exchange. We heard no more from the store and finally dropped them a line about the chair. A few days later we came home and found a chair sitting in our living room which presumably was to be exchanged for the cracked one, but it too was not the right chair. We wrote another letter. We came home a few days later and the delivery men had made their way into our house and exchanged the cracked chair with the right one. This left in our hands the wrong chair which had been placed in the living room. One day I saw the Beta Store's delivery truck and asked them to come by and pick up the chair, which they did. With that act we had what we wanted and at a very good price.

We discovered that one of the local furniture stores did carry Early Williamsburg and so I went by their store one day to compare prices. It turned out that the prices we paid were considerably lower for those items that I could compare. (They did not carry the bunk beds.) On most items the price we had paid was about 60 percent of the local price. In exchange for the low price we did have the inconvenience of a trip to the town of Beta and some problems in delivery, but the delivery was free and the credit extended without service charges.

Conclusion

I believe it would be quite accurate to say that we are quite satisfied with the furniture purchased and with the people from whom we made the purchase. The retailer, although most casual, informal, and almost lackadaisical, was straightforward in dealing with us. (His novel approach was intriguing and added some interest to the negotiations.) He sold us reputable merchandise at extremely low prices and did not hesitate at all in making whatever changes we desired in order to insure that we were satisfied with our purchase. We are, in fact, considering the purchase of some additional furniture from the Beta Store—a few single items. We have highly recommended the store to friends and acquaintances, some of whom have gone over to the store and themselves bought some merchandise. Our neighbors across the street, for example, purchased a living-room sofa, which is a very nice piece of furniture. We did not look closely at the Beta Store's living-room furniture but felt that the best buys were in dining and bedroom furniture. Our neighbor's purchase proved contrary to this conclusion.

Apparently the Beta Store has successfully built its business on selling reasonably good furniture at low prices and providing free delivery and credit without a service charge. We have, for example, yet to see an advertisement, while the Alpha Store does a great deal of advertising. Few people we know have found the Alpha Store satisfactory. Since our purchase we have heard that the Beta Store is somewhat of a sideline for its owner who, it seems, operates the town of Beta's funeral parlor. Undoubtedly, his principal income now must be from the furniture store, which sells throughout central Missouri.

Our position generally was to go along with Peter. He was fairly insistent on the style of furniture and it was pretty much in harmony with what we liked. We both felt that the particular brand that he wanted was too expensive and as far as I can tell, Peter has no particular objection to what we got. Dotty seems to think that Peter felt more strongly about the particular brand than I thought he felt. I have had no indication that the brand we got concerned him. I am sure that Dotty would have preferred the more expensive brand but there was no disagreement that the other brand was a more reasonable purchase. I believe she also agreed that it was a thoroughly satisfactory purchase. It was really an interesting purchase in that everyone's interests coincided rather closely. We're not always this fortunate.[1]

---

[1] The concluding paragraph was taken from a letter by Dr. Rigby. It seems of value in pointing out the difficulties involved in perceiving other persons' viewpoints accurately in the process of developing a group decision.

2 / Introduction to
TONIRI BUYS A HOUSE

ToNiri, a native of New Britain, entrepreneur with a number of small interests, plans to purchase a government-owned building for a house and to move it to Vunamami. His bid on the house, identical with a recent accepted bid on a similar building, is unsuccessful. Other circumstances demand his attention and he delays further consideration of a new home for almost two years.

If there is such a thing as a theory of consumer behavior, it must, of course, apply as well in islands of the Pacific as it does in Indianapolis. Salisbury, thoroughly familiar with primitive tribes, performs much of the translation into terminology suitable for a discussion of a similar purchase of a home in a developed economy.

It is probably not rare for people who have an apartment or a house to look around for one more suitable, even when there is no real necessity to purchase one. Since houses, except for new ones, generally have an asking price against which one bids; it is surely not unusual for people to make an offer and to have it refused.

Some interesting implications of this process are largely hidden, but are suggested by ToNiri's actions, which cannot be taken as typical. Having gone to considerable trouble to determine the amount to bid, having planned the movement and reconstruction of the house, ToNiri apparently postponed any further consideration of alternatives for some time after his bid was rejected. This action suggests that in some way the process of planning and bidding actually reduced the desire for a new house or partially satisfied it.

Should this be a phenomenon common to many persons and products, it raises a number of theoretical questions and may partially explain losses of sales when salesmen fail to close at the appropriate time. Is it possible that a woman who wants a fur coat strongly can partially satisfy that desire simply by visiting a store and trying on several coats? Perhaps there is some such thing as a symbolic or simulated purchase that provides a reasonable amount of the psychic satisfaction thought to accompany actual purchase.

It is not difficult to see the influence of society and culture on ToNiri's actions. Perhaps his action of bidding on the house was in itself an important development in his changing status within the village, since most of the village must have known of it. If so, it is not difficult to see that the bidding could accomplish some of the status-giving functions of actual ownership. Perhaps other consumer actions that do not culminate in purchases have functions worth examining.

TONIRI BUYS A HOUSE

Richard F. Salisbury, *Department of Sociology and Anthropology, McGill University*

On November 3, 1961, ToNiri[1] of Vunamami village in New Britain deposited a tender to buy a government-owned house in nearby Rabaul for £65 (pound), which was due for demolition to make way for new construction. Before he sent in this tender he had discussed with me in some detail his plans regarding the house, its re-erection in the village, and how he had learned about the house being available. The other factors that influenced his decision he did not explicitly discuss with me, though my knowledge of him personally and of the history of Vunamami make it clear that they were operating, even if ToNiri was not consciously aware of them. These factors provide the frame within which ToNiri worked in making his decision.

The History and Background of Vunamami

Vunamami is one of the most advanced villages of the Tolai peoples of New Britain, a group numbering almost 50,000 people, living in some 300 square miles around Rabaul. They have been part of the Australian-administered Territory of New Guinea since it ceased being a German colony in 1920. Intensive European contact began in 1875 with missionaries, traders, and planters and until 1910 the German administrative centre for New Guinea was located 2 miles from Vunamami village in Kokopo. In 1910 the centre was moved to Rabaul, 17 miles around a bay.

By 1922 Vunamami village land, much reduced by European land pur-

---

[1] ToNiri is a pseudonym. Some aspects of his personal history have been also changed to preserve his anonymity, though without affecting the validity of this study.

chases, was virtually completely planted with coconuts for cash cropping. Some villagers, the first in New Britain, had been ordained as Methodist ministers; others were working as clerks in Government offices, in addition tò the many employed as unskilled labor in nearby Kokopo. An effective local leader had organized public works, and obtained government hearing for local opinion. But between 1922 and 1935 prosperity diminished, coconut plantings fell into poor repair, education declined, and the new Australian administration disrupted the previously effective local political organization. After 1935, with the appointment of a dynamic native political leader, with progress in technical education, improvement in world markets for primary products and with the increasing administrative competence of the Australians, prosperity began to return to New Britain. This prosperity was interrupted by the war when some 70,000 Japanese occupation troops were put off in the Rabaul area, compelling the Tolai to work for them. The area was bombed daily by the allies and half the coconut palms and all buildings were destroyed.

After the Japanese capitulation in 1945, temporary buildings were hastily thrown up, but little permanent rebuilding was begun before 1950, by which time shipping, the plantation economy, and the supply of consumer goods were reapproaching normalcy. After 1950 the introduction of cocoa as a cash crop, the development of elective indigenous local government, the rise of the cooperative movement, and the introduction of schooling in English (rather than pidgin or vernacular) for all grades, accompanied a spectacular rise in personal cash incomes among the Tolai. Skilled men were in great demand throughout New Guinea at salaries approaching those prevailing in Australia; more local jobs, skilled and semiskilled, were available to village residents who could commute to work, including many positions within the native local government system; Vunamami cocoa and coconut farmers gained in the period of high-world prices following the Korean war, and the expansion of their plantings tided over the later declines in prices; even unskilled workers benefitted from increasing wage rates. The year 1961 was one of continuing expansion, despite the low prices of cocoa.

This pattern of growth in the Vunamami economy has involved many changes in the consumption demands of the area.[2] The earliest demand from traders in the 1870s was for weapons for use in the internal political

---

[2] For a more detailed description of the early changes in Tolai consumption patterns and their correlation with the stages of economic growth see R. F. Salisbury, *From Stone to Steel: Economic Consequences of a Technological Change in New Guinea.* New York: Cambridge University Press, 1962. This article also compares the Tolai changes with the virtually identical pattern for the New Guinea Siane; a theory of cyclical changes in consumption patterns is advanced. See R. F. Salisbury, "Early Stages of Economic Development in New Guinea," *Journal of the Polynesian Society*, 71, 1962, 328-339.

struggles of the time. A demand for consumer luxuries such as tobacco and cloth, umbrellas and peroxide, grew as German governmental control was established, as wealth became more widely spread, and the political struggles became a competition for bureaucratic positions. The period 1900 to 1922 saw, in addition to the demand for luxuries, an immense expansion of Vunamami investment in durable goods, both for production and for consumption. Horses and carts, boats and tree planting represented productive investments; churches with concrete foundations and metal roofs, houses of the same materials, and cemeteries with concrete memorials were the consumer durable expenditures. But by the advent of difficult times around 1923, only the two wealthiest men of Vunamami village had built houses of this type. During World War II the metal from them was commandeered by the Japanese and no more such houses were built in Vunamami until 1953. During the period 1923-1945 consumer demands dried up to the bare minimum of tobacco, rice and meat, machetes, and cloth lengths (*laplaps*), goods needed to keep society going. Whereas in 1920 most men had worn shirts and long trousers as a minimum, by 1935 the wrap-around *laplap* was the only garment used. A few men in the late 1930s, as prosperity began returning, tried to invest productively by making copra driers out of kerosene drums and corrugated iron, but their efforts too were brought to a standstill by the war. The 1950s, however, saw a pattern of consumer demand paralleling that of the period 1900-1922. Productive investment in large items like trucks, driers and tree planting was universal; the expendable consumer goods demanded were of better quality. Thus tailored kilts (termed *sulu*) usually of pearl grey, replaced *laplaps,* drip-dry white shirts replaced T-shirts, and Rothman's cigarettes replaced Craven A, as the latter had replaced twist tobacco as the "correct" thing to offer a guest to smoke. The same trend was visible in consumer durables, with ownership of bicycles, sewing machines and, in 1961, radios and cameras becoming increasingly widespread and the subject of competition to obtain a model better than one's neighbor.

Housing trends were the same. The newly constituted Local Government Council had in 1952 built its chambers and accommodation for teachers and medical assistants from war surplus materials purchased from the United States Navy base at Manus. Other surplus materials from local military camps were incorporated, somewhat haphazardly, into copra driers, house roofs and water storage tanks in combination with local uncut timbers, straw, and bamboo. But by 1955 three of the wealthiest men of Vunamami had built houses entirely of sawed timbers, composition board, and corrugated iron, raised up on concrete piers capped with termite shields. Not all members of the village could follow suit, even by 1961. At that time eight of the sixty-nine houses were so constructed, though the later houses incorporated many improvements—more ample and better floor plans, louvred glass windows for ventilation, and concrete steps not touching the walls to prevent termite entry. By 1961, too, only ten houses were built solely of native materials, while the remainder all incorporated some European features into native construction—principally some metal sheeting in the roof and a means of collecting rain water. Many houses were flanked also by a second house, under construction in the spare time of the owner, who was saving in the meantime for cash to buy the next manufactured item needed—metal sheets for the roof, or composition board for the walls. House building was the current rage.

ToNiri's Background

Let us now return to ToNiri, to consider his personal history, and how he was involved in house buying. He was born in 1926 of relatively well-educated parents, and through his mother had claims on land in Vunamami village. His father was a government clerk from a village 6 miles along the coast who saw to it that his son obtained an education up to about the seventh-grade standard in the mission schools, which taught in the vernacular. When the Japanese occupation of New Guinea began, ToNiri's father was working in Salamaua on the mainland and had his family with him. The Australian advance left them in allied territory while their relatives and village ties were in Japanese occupied New Britain. They visited the Tolai area after the capitulation, but once again ToNiri's father was posted out of New Britain, and ToNiri followed. The war had interrupted his education, and he attempted to complete it, while taking semi-trained clerical jobs. On one of his visits home he married a Tolai girl from the neighboring village of Vunabalbal, and she accompanied him as he slowly progressed as a store clerk in a large firm. His lack of English increasingly handicapped his progress, however, especially as the newer generation with uninterrupted post-war educations in English began leaving school. Nevertheless, he was a well-educated member of his own generation, highly intelligent, with more sophisticated tastes in food, clothing, and accommodation than the majority of Tolai.

His sophisticated tastes proved his downfall. He was arrested one night at a gambling party in Lae where liquor was being consumed at a time when gambling and drinking were still both against the law for native New Guineans. After his prison term he was not rehired by his employers, who also would not give him a reference to other employers. He returned in 1960 to Vunamami where he had land claims, though he had not lived there regularly for twenty years. With the help of a clan brother he quickly built a house of native materials, incorporating a metal roof and a water tank, sufficient to house his family of five—himself, his wife, his seven-year-old son, and daughters aged three and one. This was his position when I first met him—a virtual outsider to village politics, with no acreage of tree crops as all other important men had, and little familiarity with Tolai customs but with a knowledge of management and the intelligence to make him an important man; a sophisticate with standards to keep up, but without a regular income to enable him to do so. At my house he could talk freely and he impressed me with his knowledge and abilities; I was not invited back to his house. I only later found out where it was and realized how incongruous it was for him. Having a house of European type was clearly a necessity for ToNiri, given the current fashion of house buying and given his own status aspirations.

ToNiri did not discuss his housing needs with me between my arrival in Vunamami in April 1961 [3] and October when he broached the question of tendering for the government-surplus house. It was only in retrospect that the pressing nature of his status needs became evident, when, as will be described later, he told me of the events leading up to his tendering. But other aspiring men of the village with similar status needs met them differently, by building in their spare time adjacent to their temporary houses, using savings as they trickled in. Why did ToNiri not do the same? He did not discuss this subject, but from his background an answer can be given.

Firstly, it was not that he lacked the necessary skills. On his return to Vunamami in 1960 he had followed the example of several friends with a similar educational background, purchased a set of tools for about £80, and set up in business as a carpenter. At school he had acquired some carpentry skills, and through watching building work during his employment he had learned the principles of frame construction. He had worked first at assisting his established contracting carpenter friends as they built houses in Kokopo town or on nearby plantations. His self-confidence and ability to learn on the job had paid off, and in 1961 he was obtaining contracts on his own account as often as he worked helping other carpenters. Half of the carpenters in the village already had European-style houses, and the other half were building them in their spare time, so that ToNiri, with his skills, was exceptional in not so doing.

As compared with other carpenters, and with educated farmers or clerical workers, ToNiri's time expenditures were also exceptional, however, and this may explain his failure to build. Like other carpenters he spent about one-third of 1961 in paid employment, although ToNiri earned above the average amount, receiving between £150 and £200 in

[3] This fieldwork was supported by the University of California Institute of International Studies, and by the USPHS National Institute of Mental Health grant No. MH4912.

all. When ToNiri had a contract, he worked from early morning until nightfall, bicycling home in the dark, caked in perspiration. Between contracts, though, ToNiri spent most of his time planting cocoa on an area of land that he owned five miles south of Vunamami. Almost half of his working days went in this way, although no monetary return would be obtained for three years, when the cocoa trees began to bear. Other carpenters and farmers with established plantings worked less on cocoa—about one day in four—and were obtaining a steady income from plantings. The longer ToNiri put off planting, the longer he would have to wait before he would have the steady income and the alternative employment needed if the risky business of contracting was to be really profitable. Without a steady income his community status would be insecure, therefore ToNiri wished to first establish his cocoa before providing for his current expenditures.

His third main set of activities, taking about a sixth of his working time, related to copra production. He prepared copra from a small area of coconuts owned by his wife, helped fellow clansmen prepare their copra, and combined with three other fellow clansmen to build and operate a copra drier financed from combined savings. His wife drew about £17 of income from copra in 1961, but most of ToNiri's time must be interpreted as a capital investment for the future, building up a credit of obligations that would enable him to call on the assistance of others when needed for his own cocoa cultivation and copra-drier investments. In 1961 he drew no income from the drier. His wife did cultivate some subsistence food crops.

What little spare time ToNiri had in evenings or at weekends went in assiduous attendance at village meetings, young men's Bible class, church, helping in cooperative torchlight fishing, or in corvee for the church. ToNiri showed admirable public spirit, but could hardly build a house. He had presumably decided to wait until his investments paid off when he would have both the time and the money.

The Decision to Tender

On October 7, 1961 ToNiri came to me filled with enthusiasm to say that he had been told of the forthcoming competitive tendering, and to ask if I thought it a good thing. From this point it is possible to describe ToNiri's actions from his own words, and not merely from indirect inferences. At the same time, in interpreting what he said, it must be realized (as I did *not* realize at the time) that he was seeking to explain to me why he had suddenly changed his mind and was now trying to buy, rather than wait.

In a rush of words he told me how he had by chance met an old and well-educated friend from his school days in the Rabaul market. The friend, who was employed as a clerk in the District Administration Office in Rabaul, had told him of the auction that was advertised in a notice posted at the District Office. Few people were likely to see the notice so that the information was a hot tip by an insider. ToNiri had not been carried away by his enthusiasm for a hot tip, but had closely interrogated the tipster. He had learned that a mutual acquaintance, a covillager of his friend and a distant fellow-clansman of his own, had bid successfully at a recent auction. This was indeed the way that a church in another village had acquired materials for building new classrooms, two months earlier, but ToNiri had previously thought that only Europeans or groups could tender, and not individual Tolai. On this occasion the government had said explicitly that European tenders would not be accepted.

The idea that he was doing something novel, progressive, and distinctive of a man with contacts seemed uppermost in his mind, so in my efforts to give good advice to a friend I challenged him as to whether he would get value for his money. Had he considered the costs of demolition, transport, and re-erection, not to mention the possibility that the materials were in poor condition. He replied immediately that he and one carpenter assistant could demolish the house in one day of hard work. He would need to hire a truck for two days at £7 per day for the transportation from Rabaul to Vunamami; concrete for supports, the nails, and some additional timber and glass would cost £10; he had inspected for termite infestation and there was none, though a few of the fibre-boards were broken. In all, if his bid were accepted, he would have his materials on the site for less than £100; buying them from one of the big Australian companies would cost a total of over £300.

He did not continue discussing the costs but began a tirade against the big companies. He said that they charged natives more for goods than they charged Europeans, that they deceived natives about the price of goods, and that they did not like selling to natives. He felt that the government tried to help natives, who could trust the government. That was why these materials were being made available by auction to natives. I had two impressions—First, that the government sponsorship of the auction convinced him that he would obtain a genuine bargain, and secondly that by purchasing immediately from the government he would score off the big companies that would lose his eventual business thereby.

These attitudes were commonly expressed by the Tolai. All the innovations heralding the post-1950 prosperity have been government-sponsored, and Tolai welcomed the assistance towards self-government, which they have received from the Australian administration. By contrast, the attitude to the companies was ambivalent. There was a blind, but largely justified, faith in the quality of goods bought from a trading company. Men would proudly display the label in their best white drip-dry shirt to prove that it had been bought at a trading company, rather than at half the price in a Chinese store. At the same time Tolai would refuse to patronize the companies because of their treatment of non-European customers, expressing their dislike of the companies with varying degrees of vehemence.

To make a purchase at a trading company a Tolai had to submit to personal degradation. If any white customer was present, the sales clerks would ignore him; if he tried to inspect goods for quality the clerk would hustle him away, as though he was trying to steal them, or as though his touching would dirty them; when he asked for best quality goods, clerks would commonly say "I don't think you can afford them, why don't you have one of these," and would offer the lowest quality goods stocked. The store clerk may even have felt he was being kind in doing this, but was in fact being most insulting. He implied that the customer was an impecunious plantation laborer, newly arrived from a backward area for a period of indenture, with neither the money nor the knowledge to discriminate between qualities of merchandise. Tolai could forgive the favors given to European customers—the discounts to "trade" customers, and the ready extension of credit—which they do not receive, but the failure of most Europeans to recognize the pronounced class differences within New Guinea society itself was unforgivable. It implied a failure to recognize that individuals are persons. Government officials, although generally supercilious to New Guineans, were usually keenly aware of differences within New Guinea society. Tolai felt that they obtained individual treatment, if not respect, from the government and would always deal with a government agency if at all possible.

I still felt that ToNiri's attitude to trading companies was not a rational reason for purchasing so I asked him why he was tendering £65. The obvious answer came back—this was the size of the successful bid at the previous tendering. I asked whether ToNiri understood the principle of an auction. Had he considered how much more than £65 he would be prepared to pay, as other people might bid more than £65, and he would lose the house unless he bid higher? He was unconcerned about the possibility of not getting the house—a £65 bid had been successful previously; it might well be successful now. He would try bidding £65, and would lose nothing if he was unsuccessful. There might always be another auction.

I persisted, however. Was there anything special about the figure of £65? Was this the size of his savings? His offhand reply indicated that this consideration had not bulked large in his thinking. No, he had savings of just over £100 and could pay more than £65.[4] In any case, he could always call on fellow clansmen for assistance, if needed. The bid of £65 was just because that was the size of the previously successful bid. What he was saying, I felt, was that his savings and the credit system of Tolai society meant that he could reasonably pay anything from about £50 to £100 for a capital purchase, without calculating precisely what he could afford. Within some such price range, the figure paid was determined on other bases.

What I have called the credit system of Tolai society, and ToNiri called "assistance from his clan" (*vunatarai*) needs some description, to explain why, as it is overtly available to all, ToNiri felt able to use it when others did not. Each clan is named, and membership in it follows lines of matrilineal descent. Clans are dispersed, so that fellow clansmen reside in several villages, and several clans are represented in any one village—nineteen in Vunamami. However, a group of men of one clan often form a local nucleus within any one village. These men are usually brothers, sons of sisters, or related as mothers'-brothers and sisters'-sons. The largest nucleus of ToNiri's clan, Bitakoai, lived in a village five miles to the south. Two smaller nuclei lived in Vunamami, one of them center-ing round land obtained by ToNiri's mother's-mother's-brother in about 1880.

Any clan's reputation, in which clan members share vicariously, de-pends on the number of capital assets owned by clan members. These are described to nonmembers as being "of the clan." Land is the most im-portant asset but things like canoes, esoteric ceremonial knowledge, tradi-tional shell money, and such modern innovations as copra driers and trucks are all considered. A man wishing to buy an asset may go to a fellow clansman and ask for a subscription to buy, say, "a Bitakoai truck." If the subscriptions are small compared to the buyer's payment, he may own the asset, and repay the subscription at convenience or by return subscriptions if erstwhile subscribers wish to purchase an asset. Subscribers talk about "their truck" and get vicarious prestige instead of interest. Large subscriptions usually involve the setting up of an "association" (*kivung*) whereby all subscribers own the asset in common—as was the case with the Bitakoai copra drier to which ToNiri and three other men had subscribed. They may use the asset at preferential rates; profits made by hiring out the asset are accumulated and reinvested, but not distributed.

---

[4] The analysis given earlier of ToNiri's savings, their use to buy tools and for invest-ment, and the precarious balance for him between savings, current income and expendi-ture is one made *post hoc* by me. His response here indicates the sharp distinction made by ToNiri (and other Tolai) between grandiose capital expenditures and penny-pinching on current expenditures. No incongruity is felt to exist between the two; they are separate economic worlds.

Clan credit may be used only for permanent assets, but housing in Vunamami has begun to be regarded as such. In 1961 a *kivung* of another clan
was collecting the individual savings of its members, and proposed to
allot them in turn to each member to buy a house. One house was already built and another was under construction.

It must be noted that not all members of a clan contribute, nor are the
individuals who join a *kivung* necessarily close kinsmen; in the cases I
observed they tended *not* to be close kin. Use of the clan name justifies
asking for a contribution, and, for example, draws customers for a copra
drier—it provides a reputation to trade on. But individual lenders and
organizers of businesses in fact are seeking personal advantage. An effective
means of obtaining credit is available for sums up to about £100, but
the person seeking credit must convince others, as businessmen and not
relatives, that his project is financially sound. Although the availability
of credit meant ToNiri could be flexible in the size of his bid, his need
to convince others of the merit of his purchase and of his own financial
acumen meant that he was under pressure to make as low a bid as
possible, and so to make the house appear a real bargain.

Although ToNiri used the assurance of credit while others did not,
does not mean that he took more chances than others. It is true that he
had invested in a tool kit and a copra drier, but virtually every adult in
Vunamami was a member of one or more investing associations. An association of women had already, over a period of ten years, accumulated
profits from small-scale production of lime from coral until they owned a
taxi-business employing two men, and were purchasing freehold plantation land. Their profits were of the order of 30 percent of invested capital
per annum, which is the same level of profit to be expected from more
traditional investments such as canoe ownership or exclusive rights to perform dances and ceremonies.

The difference is between investors who realize these profits and those
who do not with failures being usually due to lack of organizing abilities
or to operational inefficiency. The Bitakoai copra drier, for example, made
no profit in its first six months of operation. The Bitakoai youth hired to
run it and to collect the hire charges had spent all the income on his
own gracious living, before the association started to check closely. The
house-buying association suggests too that size of investment differentiates
the successful from the unsuccessful. The first two houses were being
built for the wealthier initiators of the association, while many poorer
members were likely to lose their contributions if enthusiasm for the
association waned before their houses were built. Even for the poorer
members the risk was worth taking. Small savings that would never suffice
for a major purchase were worth risking for the slight chance of obtain-

ing a good house. ToNiri, by having savings about which he was unconcerned, was able to behave like the successful ten percent of Vunamami risk takers who are prepared to spend one-third of their income in a single venture.

A last influence on ToNiri's change of mind and decision to buy was my own presence. By October 1961 we had had many discussions about such things as the financing of fishing, the operation of copra driers and the organization of ceremonials. Would he have had the confidence to plunge into an unfamiliar world of cash financing if I had not been there to talk to him? In the nature of things, such a question cannot be answered. My own presence and our discussions of house buying, like ToNiri's encounter with his school friend in the marketplace, must be regarded as the fortuitous historical accidents that turned the statistical probability that ToNiri would buy a house, into a decision to take active steps to purchase. The long-run factors—the cyclical history of Vunamami-consumption patterns, the current affluence of the area, ToNiri's social status and aspirations, his position in the cycle of family growth, and the availability of credit—would have been the same if I had not been there. From them alone it could have been predicted that ToNiri was "in the market" for a house.

Postscript

I left Vunamami in December 1961, before the auction results. I learned later that ToNiri's bid was not successful, though I do not know what the successful bid actually was. ToNiri's house buying must then remain as a study of a consumption decision and not of a consummated purchase. But the postscript also enables us to check the foregoing analysis to see how far the factors mentioned still operate, and how far they can be reconciled with the fact that, as of December 1963, ToNiri has not made any further bids for Government-surplus housing.

Since December 1961 ToNiri has been busy. First, new lease-hold land was made available in Kokopo town, and ToNiri, on his own account, and as the assistant of other carpenters was kept busy building houses for new Chinese residents. The building boom lasted about nine months, and then ToNiri could return to establishing his cocoa plantation. In early 1963, when this was completed, a new net-fishing season began and ToNiri joined some of the outstanding Vunamami entrepreneurs (and some unskilled laborers) in a large-scale and highly successful fishing venture. After the net fishing in August 1963, he was asked by the Local Government Council to work as a salaried assistant at the village school, supervising building operations and generally helping. With the population increasing at 5.5 percent annually two new classrooms and a new teachers' house were needed yearly and ToNiri's job looked like a permanent one.

His community status has also become clearer. At my own departure ceremonies he was initiated into the traditional religious (*tubuan*) society, to mark an acceptance into the village that had grown during my stay. He had started joining in the discussions of economic policy at village meetings very much as a junior person speaking out of turn, but speaking good sense. Increasingly he had been included into the inner circle at the village discussions, at meetings of the four-village Cooperative Society, and in public discussions of the area Local Government Council. Final acceptance as an important and wealthy man in the village came with his acceptance into the fishing *kivung*. His appointment in August 1963 meant membership in the local school board, and, as evidenced by his increasing use of English, he was associating closely with the teachers.

Thus it has remained a major concern for ToNiri to have a house appropriate to an important and sophisticated man. But the need is no longer as urgent as in 1961. As ToNiri increasingly has the status itself, he has less need for the obvious symbols of it. At the same time he has suffered a severe blow to his plans—an accidental fire destroyed his maturing cocoa plantation. He has the prospect of a year of work reestablishing it and another three years before it will yield income. His income and his savings have probably dropped. But he is now no longer looking for a bargain in housing, but has started building in his spare moments an opulent European-style house next to his old house of native materials and corrugated iron. It will cost him more cash in the long run, but he will eventually have it built. His credit is good. ToNiri is indeed buying a house.

3 / Introduction to THE JAPANESE TOP

Mary attended the first week of a store opening. She went because her sister wanted to go. Her sister wanted to go because their mother felt it a social obligation since she knew the store owners. Mary, age ten, was the only member of the family to purchase anything. It was a $1 top manufactured in Japan.

The child of ten, whose social defenses are incomplete, can often shed light on processes more mature individuals report with less candor. As the respondent says, when asked why she bought the top, "Well, I just wanted something new." With an adult there is usually a more "practical" reason, sometimes one that is explained at great length and in much detail.

Of course, the little girl in this case is an apprentice consumer who didn't really want to go on the shopping trip in the first place. Money was burning a hole in her pocket. The purchase was clearly an impulse purchase, and one that is reported here fairly frankly, with considerable naiveté but not without shrewdness. It should make one wonder about the extent to which other impulse purchases have essentially the same character. The item purchased was clearly of uncertain use, and the satisfaction that has been received from the purchase and that which is yet to be received are still difficult to evaluate.

The probability that satisfaction is purely emotional and nonrational is suggested by the fact that Mary cannot really explain why she feels the purchase was satisfactory. She enjoys using the toy, but it bores her after a time. It even causes fights.

Her efforts to evaluate the product in money terms are primitive attempts to explain or rationalize price and utility. She is not at all sure whether value is tied up in production costs or in the satisfaction she derives from the item, which puts her approximately on a par with most of the rest of us.

If one holds to the concept of utility, the discussion of price and value

46

are enormously reassuring. The price paid for the top was greater than its utility to the seller and less than its stated utility to the buyer.

But perhaps the most interesting statement of the predicament of the consumer that has yet been made sums up her emotional responses in a revealing fashion. "And I thought I was really wasting my money, but now that I have it, I like it better than I thought I would—but not real good."

Cognitive dissonance? Simple uncertainty? Or the indication of an underlying hierarchy of satisfactions that is well-developed?

THE JAPANESE TOP

W. T. Tucker, *Department of Marketing, University of Texas*

Mary is a ten-year-old. She has had minor hearing problems and does not speak quite as clearly as the average ten-year-old. For this reason, and for differences in temperament, she often lets Sarah speak for the two of them when dealing with adults. Sarah is her sister, about twenty months younger. Mary probably has the greater self-confidence. She is extremely matter-of-fact. She states that she was probably shy without a trace of shyness.

The occasion referred to occurred when Mary's mother went to visit a newly opened gift shop and specialty store, owned by acquaintances she had known a relatively short time. The visit was, therefore, primarily social and was not a shopping trip.

Q: Mary, I'd like you to tell me about this little top. When did you buy it?

Mary: About two weeks ago.

Q: Where did you get it?

Mary: I think at the (X's) store. I don't know. (She is not sure of the name of the owner.)

Q: How come you bought this top?

Mary: Well, I just wanted something new. Well, see, I went to the store and, I just—you know, wanted something new. And I was kind of disappointed because you know, all the things they had were about fifty dollars. And I was kind of looking and I found that, and I thought it would be real expensive, but it was only a dollar and so I, well, I just wanted it. I didn't think I would you know, have much fun with it, but I just wanted it—cause I just wanted something new.

Q: When you say most of the things you saw in the store were fifty dollars, you mean they were things you wanted too?

Mary: No.

Q: They weren't? What do you mean by that?

Mary: Well, some of them were, but . . .

Q: Some were like what?

Mary: Well, they were things like desks, and I don't want one of those.

Q: Desks? And what else?

Mary: Well, there was an antique stool with a wood carrier on it, and I don't need that.

Q: Did you see anything else that you did like?

Mary: Well, there was this thing and it had, well, it was a back scrubber, you know. You couldn't tell what it was unless someone explained it to you. There were these, well, you can't explain it too well.

Q: A back scrubber?

Mary: Yes, it's an itcher, kind of, and you . . . .

Q: Oh, you mean one that you scratch your back with. Back scratcher?

Mary: Oh, I don't know, just for kind of, back . . . to make you feel good.

Q: No, uh, it wasn't one you use in the bath?

Mary: No, it was wood.

Q: It was one you just scratch your back with.

Mary: Yes.

(Actually this was a back-massage unit, made of straps, wooden balls, and the like—somewhat difficult to describe.)

Q: Why did you go to this store?

Mary: Well, Mom wanted to see it and Sarah wanted to go with her. I really didn't want to go, but I didn't have anything else to do, so I just went to see what they had there and everything. And if I wanted anything, I could go to others.

Q: How did you pay for this?

Mary: Well, I won the fifty dollar door prize (at a bingo games party), you know, and I had some money left over. I bought two dresses, but I had some money left over and I bought it with that.

Q: How much money did you have left over?

Mary: Fourteen dollars and thirty-three cents.

Q: And this top only cost one dollar. Right? Was it the only thing you saw there that didn't cost very much?

Mary: Well, some things cost . . . well, there was this little bag there that cost eight dollars.

Q: A little what?

Mary: A bag you carry, you know, just anything you want to like at a beach resort. You just have a little bag. A cloth bag. And there was a trash can, but I didn't want a trash can. It cost a dollar. That's about all that was cheap.

Q: Why did you want to go with your Mother and Sarah?

Mary: I didn't really. You see, Sarah kind of talked me into it.

Q: What would you have done if you hadn't gone?

Mary: Just played at home.

Q: Do you have any idea why she wanted to go?

Mary: Well, she . . . this lady was, you know, at our party and she came to talk to Sarah and she (Sarah) wanted to see if it was the same woman at the store.

Q: I see. Have you liked having the top?

Mary: Pretty much.

Q: What do you mean by that?

Mary: Well, you don't really . . . all you do is see it spin around.

Q: You mean you'd sell it to somebody else now for a dollar?

Mary: Probably.

Q: Probably?

Mary: Yeah, I thought I was kind of wasting my money.

Q: Have the other kids played with it very much?

Mary: Yes. We have kind of races with it, you know, and that's how that thing got there on the side, that wood chipped off. It always runs into things

Q: What do you mean you have races with it?

Mary: Well, see, we see how far each one can spin it, you know. That's how we have races with it.

Q: How do you tell how far it goes?

Mary: Well, when it just comes up there—usually Peggy, she comes and just marks it where it is.

Q: Is that where it ends?

Mary: No, it usually goes . . . well, see it usually comes up at a place, then it goes back down, but we mark how far it goes up.

Q: I notice the string on it got broken.

Mary: Yes.

Q: What was wrong with it?

Mary: Well, see, uh, Jean pulled it with her fingers and she got it out, but I don't know how she got it out, you know, there was a knot at the end so you couldn't put it back or anything, and I couldn't fix it because there was a knot at the end, so I cut that off and then I just stuck it through and tied a knot.

Q: Uh huh. And you put this wax on the end, so that you could get it through.

Mary: Didn't work too well, though.

Q: How did you do that?

Mary: Well, I got a short candle that we didn't need anymore, and I got a piece of paper, and I lit the candle and just let the wax drip on it.

Q: On the string. And that made the end of it stiff enough so that you could get it through this little handle?

Mary: Uh huh.

Q: Do you fix a lot of things when they're broken?

Mary: Yep. And I like to.

Q: Sounds to me like that's the kind of thing that a boy does, not the kind of thing that a girl does.

Mary: Well, maybe I was just—I don't know—maybe I was supposed to be a boy and just turned out a girl.

Q: Well, I don't think there's anything wrong with a girl doing it, do you?

Mary: No. I would really like to be a boy, kind of.

Q: You would?

Mary: Uh huh.

Q: What do you mean—kind of?

Mary: Well, I like being a girl and everything, but I don't know, I'd just like to be a boy, but not when he was young. I'd like to be a girl when I was young and a man when I grew up.

Q: You would. What do you mean by young? You mean like you?

Mary: Yeah.

Q: You'd rather be a girl now, but you'd like to be a boy when you grow up.

Mary: Right when I'm—well, right now I'd like to change into a boy, I guess.

Q: About now?

Mary: About the beginning of the fifth grade.

Q: Is there anything in particular you like about this top?

Mary: Well, not really. Well, kind of. I don't know.

Q: What do you mean—kind of?

Mary: I just like it . . . well, I like it . . . I don't know.

Q: Do you play with it very much?

Mary: Uh huh. I get bored.

Q: You play with it a good deal, but you get bored. What does that mean? Does that mean you spin it some and then you stop?

Mary: Well, all you do is spin it, and there's nothing to do after you spin it, unless you race it—that's the fun part.

Q: Little hard to have a race with just one top, though, isn't it?

Mary: Uh huh. We always fight over it.

Q: You fight over it. Now what do you mean by that?

Mary: Well, Sarah says her turn is next, and it's really Sally's or Peggy's or something like that. And then, maybe well, we just get in a fight. And we end it when, well, I don't know, we just—someone says it's their turn and it's really someone else's and then someone gets mad because I tell someone to, you know, it hits this thing and scars it all up, and I tell someone to put a pillow by it and they won't. So I put it by it and they want to lie on the pillow and, you know, and I say, "O.K., here." But I don't really give it to them, and then they get in a fight and just fight like that.

Q: Uh huh. Do they argue very much about who won when they have races with it?

Mary: No.

Q: Why do you suppose they don't?

Mary: Well, because you can, well, the top doesn't go as far. Well, it's just not a little way apart, you know, when it ends, it's usually by a yard or two, because some people can't spin it right you see.

Q: Who normally wins?

Mary: Me.

Q: You. Why is that—because it's your top?

Mary: I don't know, maybe it likes me. I guess I just have more practice than them.

Q: Tell me, how much do you think this top is worth?

Mary: Right now, or when it was new?

Q: Well, when it was new.

Mary: About one dollar and seventy-five cents.

Q: About one dollar and seventy-five cents?

Mary: A little more than that.

Q: And what do you think that it's worth right now?

Mary: One dollar and twenty-five cents.

Q: One dollar and twenty-five cents. And how much did you pay for it?

Mary: One dollar.

Q: One dollar. Why do you think they sold it to you for one dollar when it was worth one dollar and seventy-five cents?

Mary: Cause most of the things in there were expensive and maybe they thought they'd get money off of those; I don't know. Maybe they just thought it was worth a dollar.

Q: They only thought it was worth a dollar, but you thought it was worth one dollar and seventy-five cents. Why do you say one dollar and seventy-five cents?

Mary: Because, I don't know, because . . . it seems like to make it would be kind of hard.

Q: How was it made?

Mary: Don't ask me. I don't know.

Q: Well, when you look at it, what do you see about it?

Mary: Well, they probably got a piece of wood and got, I guess, some mold or something, and got a machine that would, well, they got a machine that would cut like that. . . . That couldn't be right. . . . Well, they probably got a machine that would, on that part, they'd probably get one that, you know, goes slanted outwards, you know.

Q: Now that's the top itself?

Mary: And then there where that would be, the end, already. They'd probably just smooth it out and smooth that all out.

Q: And then, how about the handle that the top sits in?

Mary: You mean, this?

Q: Uh huh.

Mary: Well, they probably just got, uh, a piece of wood about that size and cut a hole in it. Well, they had to take all that bulk off and everything. You know that. And make a hole, I mean and punch a hole through the other side.

Q: Do you know where this top comes from?

Mary: Japan, I think.

Q: And do you think as you look at it and you see all the work that was done, uh, that it really was worth about one dollar and seventy-five cents?

Mary: (nods)

Q: Well, is there anything else about this that you can tell me about? What you do with it, or what you might do with it later on?

Mary: Can I tell you something else first?

Q: Sure.

Mary: Well, uh, the reason I said it would be about one dollar and seventy-five cents, it might be less, because now that I look at it, it looks more easily to make, and one thing, if I got it for one dollar and seventy-five cents, I would only sell it for just a little less than that because well, you could get just about as much as I would out of it. . . .

Q: In other words, it isn't used up and it isn't particularly hurt, except for that one little place where it's been nicked some, huh?

Mary: Uh huh, that's the way with anything, I mean, if you had it for a pretty long time and still it isn't too beaten up unless its a wreck, you could get some use out of it, but it's already used so you would sell it for just a little less.

Q: You wouldn't want to sell it for too much less? What would you sell it for right now?

Mary: Well, a dollar or so. Wait, let's see. $1.25 probably.

Q: One dollar and twenty-five cents? That's more than you paid for it, though, isn't it?

Mary: I thought that all along in the first place. (That is was *worth* more than the dollar price.)

Q: Oh. Do you think that you have had a dollar's worth of fun out of this top?

Mary: Now that I think of it, I wouldn't sell it for one dollar and twenty-five cents.

Q: Well, do you think that you and the other girls together have had a dollar's worth of fun out of it?

Mary: Well, I guess I have had a dollar's fun out of it. I'm not—Well, pretty much a dollar's fun out of it.

Q: Pretty much a dollar's fun, huh? What do you intend to do with it now?

Mary: Play with it, and when it gets worn out, well, I usually just save things, and when I'm making things or something like that, I could use one of those pieces, when it's all broken up or something, and part of it is still left. I usually can just use one of those pieces or something, and I save it in my junk drawer.

Q: I see, you'd use it for something else?

Mary: Now I wouldn't; but, you know, when it was all banged up or wouldn't work anymore.

Q: Do you expect that you'll be using it as much right now as you have been for the last week or so? (Mary shakes head) No? Why not?

Mary: Well, because, when I first got it I wasn't used to it or anything and like when I had a pet or something, like my snake, I used to always play with him cause I hadn't seen him before too much, and now I just let him go for a day and don't even see him. That's the same with the top. When I got it, I liked it and everything and played with it a whole lot, but then after a while, I got used to it.

Q: So now you don't play with it quite as much as you used to? But you expect you will still play with it some, I imagine?

Mary: Uh huh.

Q: And then finally, when it gets broken, you'll save the pieces in your drawer? What did you call that, your "junk drawer?"

Mary: Uh huh.

Q: Do you have a lot of things in your junk drawer?

Mary: Uh huh. I have to have two junk drawers.

Q: You have to have *two* junk drawers?

Mary: No, I have three. Well, one—there isn't too much in it. Yes, I have two, but they're just little.

Q: Mary, can you remember much more about buying that top?

Mary: Yes, there was the man, Mr. (what was his name)?

Q: Rudd?

Mary: (continuing) Rudd and Sarah picked it up and she was asking Mom what it was, and she said it was a top, and I didn't tell anyone, but you know I thought in my head about it, and I wanted it, and so the man came over and Sarah asked the man what it was and he was showing it to her, and she was showing it to Sarah, and all; he was spinning it and showing us how to wind it up. He said that—he was telling us this story about his wife and his dog, or something like that, that you know, his dog couldn't catch it, and had a lot of fun out of it. I was thinking that I really didn't want it, but I wanted something new, and so I just decided I had enough money left over just to get that. And I thought I was really wasting my money, but now that I have it, I like it better than I thought I would, but not real good.

Q: What did you say to the man?

Mary: Sarah did most of the talking. Really, I just stood and watched her.

Q: Well, I mean when you decided you wanted it. Did you ask him to wrap it up for you?

Mary: Well, see, I asked Mom if I could buy it. She said, "Are you sure?" and I said, "Uh huh." The man, I guess he thought I was going to change my mind, he hurried back and got a new top and wrapped it and everything, so I couldn't change my mind or anything like that. After I had just said "Yea, well I guess so," well he just went and got a box and went back there until I could change my mind, but I wasn't going to, but you know he thought I would. He gave it to me and I told him, "Thank you."

Q: Why did you ask your mother?

Mary: Well, I wouldn't just go off and buy something and have her never know about it.

Q: It was your money, wasn't it?

Mary: Yeah, I guess I was kind of shy.

Q: Kind of shy?

Mary: Yes, I guess Mom should have known about it before he did. I would have asked him, but I guess Mom should have known about it before he did.

Q: I see, so you asked her before you told him, right?

Mary: Uh huh, I asked her and she said, "Are you sure?" And I said, "Yes."

Q: So you really didn't tell the man you wanted it. Your mother told him that you wanted it, is that right?

Mary: Well, I think, see, he heard us. She (Sarah) said, "She wants to buy it," or something like that, and she (Mom) said, "Are you sure you want it," and I said, "Well, I guess so." And he just hurried back and got one.

Q: Your mother asked you whether you were sure you wanted it. Then when you said yes, he went back and got it, right?

Mary: Uh huh.

Q: And then he wrapped it up?

Mary: And put it in a box.

Q: Put it in a box.

Mary: In a bag.

Q: And then the box in a bag.

Mary: Uh huh.

Q: And then who did he give it to?

Mary: Me.

Q: He gave it to you?

Mary: Uh huh.

Q: Did he say anything when he gave it to you?

Mary: He said to come back.

Q: He said to come back?

Mary: Yea, I think he wanted me to buy more stuff. When I told him that I had won fifty dollars; and so he patted me on the shoulder and told me to come on back and all that.

Q: All that?

Mary: He was just teasing me, I think.

4 / Introduction to THE PURCHASE OF THREE BICYCLES

Professor McGee is a thorough shopper. He discusses here the procedures of purchasing three bicycles, one for his daughter, one for his son, and one for himself. He is obviously concerned with examining the market carefully, determining all of the products available, and making the most satisfactory selection in each case.

Some purchasers behave in what might be considered a rational or practical manner. Having assessed the function of the article they wish to purchase, they spend a considerable amount of time gathering information about alternatives. This is not an easy task. Even the process of getting in touch with suppliers and finding out product availability can take a considerable amount of time. Comparing products against price differentials is even more difficult since no two features are exactly comparable and many of the central questions relate to future conditions rather than present ones. With any sort of machinery the length of useful life and the cost of repairs, for instance, are always problematic.

It seems unlikely that anyone actually calculates the value of his time and effort as a part of the purchase price. In all probability the amount of time and effort given the process are determined by other factors such as the relative energy of the individual and his set of values. The thorough searcher might be one of three types of people, or some combination thereof.

First, there are surely people who enjoy the shopping process. For them, one cannot speak of the time and effort spent as a part of the purchase cost, since they get satisfaction even without making a purchase.

Second, there are undoubtedly people to whom the expenditure of money requires a moral justification. For them, the unwarranted expenditure of money is not merely uneconomic, it is sinful. In a country with Puritan traditions it is not unlikely that most persons have some moral qualms involved in the self-indulgence and waste that may characterize a purchase.

Third, some people seem to regard shopping as a game. You win when you get the lowest price for the most useful product. You lose the rest of the time. McGee's purchases are excellent ones against which to test the notions of economic rationality.

It may also be interesting to note the way in which he is training his son to disregard the "tail fin" aspects of products or to try to understand why the mother plays no part in the purchase of either child's bicycle. In the case of the daughter's bicycle, the circumstance is one seldom discussed in the marketing literature, but perhaps more common than one would imagine. The product is paid for by X, purchased by Y and used (or not used) by Z. Does this suggest any ways in which thinking about consumer behavior should be organized?

THE PURCHASE
OF THREE BICYCLES

Reece McGee, *Department of Sociology, Macalester College*

While I do not believe I am what might ordinarily be called a consumer of bicycles, I have had occasion to purchase three of the machines in the past two years. Each purchase was motivated by a different need and differing attitudes on my part with the result that the actual procedures of purchasing likewise differed considerably. The first two were birthday gifts for my eleven-year-old daughter and eight-year-old son. In these cases the funds were supplied by doting grandparents for whom economy was no object, while the actual selection and purchase of the machines was left to me. In the third case I was selecting a machine for my own use, and cost considerations entered the calculation. These differing sources of funds seem upon reflection to account in large part for the manner in which the purchases were made, along with, in the case of the children's bikes, my estimates of the uses to which the machines would be put.

The Girl's Bicycle

My "consumer behavior" in the purchase of the bicycle for my daughter can probably be accounted for largely under the concept of economic rationality. The grandparents who were supplying the funds for the machine have always subscribed to the mythology (I suppose middle-class in origin) that every child ought to have a bicycle. They had bought her a 20-inch sidewalk bike when she was five and now, for her tenth birthday, were determined that she must have a full-sized machine. My own estimate of the situation was otherwise, for I had observed that even though we lived in one of the older areas of the city where there were sidewalks upon which bicycles might be ridden, the child failed to take any particular advantage of the fact and seemed, indeed, largely indifferent to the whole proposal. That she might ever want a bike to ride to school was beyond consideration; her anxieties about traffic (or anything else not already thoroughly understood and familiar) precluded the possibility entirely. When some tentative suggestion of these feelings about the matter produced only calumny heaped upon my head by the grandparents (only an unnatural father could believe a child would not be thrilled by a new bicycle!), I decided simply to buy her the cheapest full-sized machine it was possible for me to find in the city, thus providing the child the opportunity her grandparents were determined she should have while saving them as much waste in their investment as possible.

When the money arrived I checked the Montgomery Ward, Sears-Roebuck, Western Auto, and Firestone catalogues on the assumption that their machines would prove cheapest, and then, using the Yellow Pages, telephoned every other retail bicycle outlet in the city. It did not at that time (nor, indeed, at any other until the moment of this writing), occur to me to inquire at the University Co-Op from which it is sometimes possible for faculty members to obtain considerable discounts on ordered merchandise. To my surprise, I discovered that a downtown department store offered the best price in town on 26-inch bicycles, beating even the several discount houses by $5 to $10. The following afternoon the girl and I journeyed down to view the machines on display, found a lightweight to her liking in the lowest price class ($26), and bought it.

There had, of course, been some previous consultation between my daughter and me concerning the nature of the machine to be purchased. She had never ridden a full-sized bike, happening to have no friends possessing them. She had been exposed to mine for years, to be sure, but, frightened by the horizontal frame member, the height at which the seat was set, the gear shift and unfamiliar hand brakes, had never asked nor attempted to ride it. She had looked at some of the catalogues with me and occasionally examined bikes passed on the street, but her general indifference to details of construction and ornamentation plus her total mechanical ignorance limited her requirements to two. The bicycle had to be blue (her favorite color at the time) and she thought she would prefer a lightweight like my own but with a coaster brake and without gearing.

Excepting only her demand for the color blue and her preference for a lightweight, the purchase was entirely motivated by consideration of the lowest possible cost for a machine of the size needed. I discarded as irrelevant all questions of style, trim, accessories, and origin, and followed through doggedly on my original determination to spend as little as possible. Selling in this instance was immaterial. We entered the store, went straight to the toy department, and had selected the machine we (I) wanted before a salesperson had appeared on the scene. That individual, an elderly gentlewoman who clearly knew nothing of bicycles, was content to take the order and accept my check exactly as if I were purchasing a baseball, and made no attempt to sell us a different model or accessories. It would have made no difference (except to irritate me) if she had. For the child, who has used the machine exactly as much (or as little) as I foresaw, the procedure seems to have been entirely satisfactory. I cannot say the same for myself nor, I am sure, would the grandparents be satisfied if they were aware of the following facts. Since the time of the purchase I have learned through experience that the reason for the bike's excessively low price is that it is a cheap, in all senses, Czech export model, and that both the materials from which it is made and the quality of its workmanship leave much to be desired. The frame, apparently, is of soft aluminum rather than steel, and is easily bent. The fenders appear to be constructed of tin. I have had to replace both tires as a result of splitting in the tread rubber, and neither tube retained air for more than four days at a time despite being liberally filled with a patented stop-leak I had often used successfully as a child. The chrome plating on wheels and spokes was very thin and has almost entirely rusted away, and the leather of the saddle is fast flaking apart despite repeated saddle soapings. In one sense, then, the purely economic rationality of the purchase produced minimally the results desired: the child was satisfied and has a machine adequate for her few uses of it; the demands of the grandparents that she have it were fulfilled. The marginal utility value of the approach—if I understand that concept—seems, however, to have been low.

The Boy's Bicycle

The "set" with which I approached the purchase of a bicycle for my son, almost two years later when he was eight, could perhaps be best described as one of determined parental autocracy, and was strongly influenced by my experience with the girl's bike. Again the funds for the purchase were supplied by the grandparents, this time with the understanding that while not unlimited, any reasonable amount (say up to $50) would be forthcoming. Several considerations determined the limits of possibility in this event: I now knew that the very cheapest machine in terms of purchase price was apt to be somewhat more expensive in the long run; I felt that for an active and somewhat careless boy a sturdy bicycle was a necessity (which eliminated from consideration both foreign and domestic three-geared lightweights which tend, relative to the standard American coaster-brake models, to be under-braked and delicate of adjustment). In view of the probability of future needs for repair, an American make seemed preferable to a foreign one, and finally the child himself had rather definite ideas about the kind of machine he wanted. The bicycle had to be red, and he would have greatly preferred an imported three-speed lightweight just like my own.

We spent some preliminary time with the catalogues again for the purpose of acquainting me with his ideas and demands and in order to give me an opportunity to turn his attention to the type of machine I thought more suitable for him. In this trial run at selection I was able to convince him that a three-speed lightweight would be impractical for him and that a balloon-tired bike with a coaster brake (that is, a standard American model) was desirable. He was enthralled with the gaudier and more expensive pieces such as the Schwinns, full of headlights, frametanks, horns, and so forth, but I rather suspected that these "tail-fin" aspects of the machines would be forgotten when he faced an actual bike on a sales floor. (While I had no objection in principle to these fancier pieces, they were too expensive and I knew from childhood experience of my own how useless—and how quickly ignored—the "built-in" accessories were.)

My guess concerning his reaction proved to be entirely prophetic when, following a newspaper advertisement of a bicycle sale, we went to the Montgomery Ward retail store and there found row upon row of shiny red bicycles of standard form without the nonessential accessories that had so caught his eye in the catalogues. I had only to point one out to him with the suggestion that he like it and the deed was done. The additional purchase of a wire basket (which he suggested would permit him to "run errands to the store for Mommy") satisfied his desire for accessories. Again the presence of a salesperson proved to be largely irrelevant. We had first approached a salesman at an outdoor display of the machines and been directed inside to the sporting goods department for the actual sale. The selection of the bike was in fact made from the outside group, but had we been permitted to buy it there, the basket would not have caught the boy's eye, there being no accessories displayed in that location. Once inside we had time to locate the machine he wanted, and for him to spot the basket before the busy clerks could give us their attention. In his first approach to us the inside salesman attempted to direct us to the more expensive pieces, but when I indicated we had already made a selection, he immediately desisted. His effort to make a "tie-in" sale was stopped by my interruption of him in mid-flight with the information that we had what we had come for. (I despise being "sold" things, preferring to buy or select for myself using the salesperson simply as a reference.)

The total spent in this transaction was about $30 and seems to have purchased a more reliable machine than the lower price bought for the girl. While I believe the bike may actually have been constructed in Japan, it follows American practice in having a heavy tubular steel frame and good sheet steel in the fenders and well-finished wheels. The enamel is standing up very well and the rubber and brake are of American make and are clearly superior to their counterparts on the Czech bike. Again both child and grandparents are satisfied, but this time the higher quality of the purchase had made me happier as well.

The Man's Bicycle

As I have already indicated, I am myself a bicyclist of long standing. As a child I had been bought a second-hand, 24-inch model for my eighth birthday and, having ridden the wheels off it, a new 26-inch model for my tenth. This I had ridden, discarding luggage racks, fenders, and so forth, all over the country, until I was sixteen.

In the course of these experiences, which had included some cross-country bike travel and, more importantly, in high school an 8-mile daily average to and from school and job, I had learned that a bike was a very useful form of transportation in all but the most inclement weather. There is no parking problem, ever, with a bike; its cost of operation is minimal, and further, in heavy city traffic it is often quicker than a car. (The bike rider does not get stuck in traffic jams and he can ignore stop signs, although not cross-traffic, with impunity. If the streets are just too crowded he has the sidewalks and alleys and can take shortcuts, across block-sized parks, for example, impossible to a motorist. His major danger is that a motorist, in the United States at least, does not really consider his machine a vehicle and often "does not see it," or chooses to ignore it and him.)

I had owned no bike between the ages of sixteen to twenty-three but found myself in graduate school on the G.I. Bill then and facing an impossible situation. My finances were precarious and, while I had to maintain a car for my main job and the marketing, I could not afford to drive it to the university, which charged commercial rates in its parking lots in an attempt to solve *its* parking problem through reduction of demand. On-the-street parking was out of the question for reasons of scarcity and parking meters. I lived 8 miles from the campus and the public transportation, in addition to being extremely slow and inconvenient, was more expensive than driving and parking. For a time, when I first returned to school from the Army, I hitchhiked. (Before the Army I had driven, parking in a university-owned-but-free mudhole and scaling a cliff to get to classes. The intervening years had seen the cliff staired and the mudhole paved and charged for. But hitchhiking was hazardous at best and, when I took a second job at the university and had to punch a time-clock, it was too unreliable.)

At this juncture it had occurred to me to buy a bike. There were very few on campus at that time but an older student friend of mind had one he rode the few blocks from his apartment, and his praise for the speed and grace of his English bike put me in the mind to try it. I watched the classified ads (knowing I could not afford a new machine of that variety) and at length was able to buy a fine Raleigh touring model from a high-school student, shamelessly beating down his deserved asking price from $40 to $25. I was immensely proud of the machine and my self-satisfaction knew no bounds when I discovered (after some practice) that, given the distance from my office I had had to park my car, I could get from home to office five minutes faster on the bike. I rode the Raleigh for three years thereafter, becoming a confirmed bicyclist despite the dominant American conviction that adults do not ride bikes as serious vehicles—perhaps because to do so flaunts the norm that we should endeavor to appear financially successful. I foolishly sold the machine upon graduation and have always regretted doing so. I have been unable to afford another half so fine since.

Not long after the time I bought the machine for my son I was faced with the necessity of buying another for myself when my old one (an ancient French lightweight I had paid too much for second-hand through inability to raise the price of a new one at the time) was stolen. When the theft occurred I had greeted it as providential since it gave me the longed-for opportunity to replace the old machine with a new English model. I could, of course, have done so at any time during several years before the loss of the old one, but had been unable to bring myself to spend the necessary sum so long as the old bike was still usable. The French bike was stolen in the spring; when the police had not succeeded in locating it by autumn, I felt morally justified in the purchase of a new one. My selection of the replacement was dominated by nonrational elements.

I had in mind a Raleigh touring model like one I'd owned in graduate school. During the summer in another city I had priced them, however, and learned that a replacement for that lost jewel would cost in the neighborhood of eighty dollars, a price I could not justify paying for a machine I would ride only a mile to and from my office. I had also learned that the same company made a cheaper export model that sold for around $50, and this I resolved to have.

In September when I sought to find one, however, it turned out there were none to be had in my home town. No store stocked the Raleigh and the one bicycle shop of which I knew discouraged me from ordering it through their obvious indifference. (Their main trade is locksmithing.) Further inquiry disclosed that no place in town stocked English bicycles of any make. At this time I recalled having seen some in the department store where I had bought the girl's bike at the time of that transaction. A call there told me, however, that they were stocked only for the Christmas trade and could not be expected until late November. Discouraged, I decided I might have to buy another kind, and began to make the rounds of stores once more, this time seeking any three-speed lightweight. I checked the department stores, Wards, Sears, Western Auto, and Firestone, and called the discount houses. There was something wrong with every machine I saw. Most were gaudy red and white and I would have (God knows why!) none else than black. Many were Japanese, and I did not trust their gearing (again without reason or evidence). The Sears store carried an altogether lovely Austrian machine but I did not like the configuration of its finger shift. (In retrospect it appears that I was determined to have an English bike or none.) The salesmen to whom I spoke in the course of this quest were universally ignorant of bicycles in general and of the construction and characteristics of the machines they tried to sell me in particular. Some were obnoxiously insistent in the affirmation of what I knew to be their ignorances, and one or two had clearly never even ridden bicycles themselves. I finally gave up and decided to wait until December when I would be able to buy one from the department store downtown.

Only a few days after that decision I discovered, quite by accident, a tiny bicycle shop near one of the parks in town. I had known of its existence from the Yellow Pages and had even seen it, but from its hovel-like appearance and piles of rusting parts and rental bikes had unthinkingly discarded it from consideration. Passing it one day, however, I stopped on impulse to inquire. The owner was absent working at some other job (he could not possibly have made his living from his bikes), but his wife opened a lean-to storage shed where gleamed exactly the machine I had been seeking. It was in the same price and quality class as the Raleigh export model I had concluded I must have and, while a brand I had never heard of, was the black-and-white English lightweight my heart was set on. I returned that afternoon and bought it.

The owner, present this time, was an elderly German who clearly knew his bikes and made it plain to me I was getting an inferior machine, and would be well to buy the expensive Raleigh I told him I yearned for, but told me also he refused to stock them, or even the cheaper models, because they were unappreciated in Texas. He said, in effect, that the bike I was buying was good enough for Texans and for me, although he did allow it was the best in town and for the price ($49) a quality machine. Events have proved him accurate. It has been entirely satisfactory, indeed excellent, mechanically, although some of the subsidiary features (quality of saddle, gauge of steel in handlebars), are less than perfect. Thus, despite my accidental location of the machine and impulsive and not entirely rational purchase thereof, I remain thoroughly satisfied if not ecstatic with it.

Summary

Much of the sociological content of the above materials is relatively self-evident in them, but one facet common to the three purchases is somewhat less than obvious and may have theoretical significance in the understanding of consumption as a social process. This is the near total irrelevance of the seller, or sales personnel, in each of the three events, and the lack of social interaction between such "sellers" and myself in the sales process. It is apparent in the descriptions that the clerk or sales person functioned, really, not as a person at all, but rather as a *process* for the acceptance of payment and delivery of merchandise. The reasons why this was so are plain. In the cases of the children's bicycles, my dominant role was as an intermediary between the children and the grandparents and was, thus, primarily a function of my *kinship* status that had nothing to do with the mercantile establishment. In my own case my demand for a black-and-white English lightweight, together with the financial limitations upon the purchase and the lack of such machines in town, restricted the sales process to one source and one machine. (There is, of course, a social or cultural limitation operative in this instance as well: English bicycles were simply *not* available for sale in my city although lightweights of other origins are sold here in large numbers.) There were, thus, four sets of limitations operating in these situations, all of which made it impossible for a salesperson to effectively influence the outcomes of the events. Given the financial limits in each of the three purchases, a number of machines were automatically excluded. Given my role in the purchase of the children's bikes as an essentially familial and parental one, my assumed responsibility to defend the grandparents from excessive expenditure and to define the utilities the children would have for the machines and buy accordingly again excluded much latitude in "selling" us machines. Further, I had narrowed the range of potential or permissible purchase considerably before ever appearing on a sales floor. In my own case my emotional demands determined that only one machine in the city qualified as a possible purchase. All of these conditions operating together made it next to impossible that any clerk would significantly affect the nature of the purchase to be made by his presence or suggestions since, in effect, nearly all the relevant decisions had been made ahead of time. The situations were so totally defined before my appearance in the store that manipulation by the clerk was impossible, and his role, therefore, became that of a mere receiver of money and purveyor of merchandise.

This situation seen in many varieties of retail endeavor is, of course, explicitly recognized in the serve-yourself-shopping pattern already institutionalized in supermarkets, discount houses, dime stores, and so forth. This suggests that there may be some kinds of commodities where retail "selling" is inefficient or even wasteful: those where product differentiation, brand loyalty, or essential simplicity permit the customer to be his own salesman. For other types of purchase, for example, houses or cars, it is possible that the relation established between salesperson and customer remains an effective instrument of marketing, but further customer role-analysis might show it to be superfluous here as well. In still others, for example, those enterprises such as gasoline stations that sell a *service* as well as a product, it is plain that most customers cannot substitute themselves as salesmen. (The do-it-yourself station now appearing sells only the product and the average customer is incapable of, or unwilling to perform, the service.)

Introduction to
A SHIRT FOR JUAN NAVARRO

Juan Navarro is a Mexican peasant who purchases a "good" shirt when his best shirt becomes too tattered to wear to town. He is unfamiliar with stores, distrusts merchants, and lives just one step above a primitive subsistence level. He gets work from a visiting archeologist and visits town to replace his worn, good shirt on payday.

What do purchases mean to the poor? Is the process as traumatic and frightening as Juan's experience seems to have been? In no case in this book does the strange, magnetic field in which the purchaser and product are momentarily suspended so clearly emerge. Nowhere is the consumer's inability to cope with the marketing institutions and the purchasing process so well-stated. It is possible, of course, to think of this as the peculiar inability of an uneducated Mexican to cope with a particular element of his own culture. But it may generalize for the poor, the illiterate, the inexperienced of all nations.

There is no inherent reason why a theory of consumer behavior should concern itself with the quality of the purchaser's experience. Nor is there any reason that this should be presumed to lie outside such a theory. There is considerable evidence that the poor get less quality for their money than other elements of society, in part for a number of reasons having to do with institutional character. For instance, interest on credit is frequently highest in institutions that are most readily available to the poor; guarantees and return privileges are likely to be honored in the breach in stores that serve them. And, conversely, the attractiveness of the product possibly blinds the have-nots to the impracticality of its acquisition in ways not encountered by those accustomed to higher material standards of living.

None of this would be of major import if it were not for the possibility that everyone is a bit of a Juan Navarro under some circumstances. The new home purchaser, the young man looking for an engagement ring, the novice buying his son fishing equipment—any of these may find the purchasing process a difficult maze for which their experience ill prepares them.

And the tyro attempting to buy an antique or a painting may well find the matter beyond his ability.

As if to emphasize the nature of the purchasing problem, it is not Juan Navarro, but Chauncey Vincent (in "Purchasing and Living with a Swimming Pool") who pays an unexpected $900 additional for a product with a serious flaw. More able to sustain and rationalize such shocks, Vincent does not feel disenfranchised or disoriented, perhaps because he understands the uncertainties of a market society.

Theorizing about consumer behavior seldom dwells upon the impact of marketing upon the consumer or the ways in which its institutions impinge upon his daily life. Yet it would seem strange to eliminate this whole range of effects from consideration. Obviously, analysis of this entire area calls for more sophisticated views than a simple categorizing of favorable and unfavorable consequences.

A SHIRT FOR JUAN NAVARRO

Jeremiah F. Epstein, *Department of Anthropology, University of Texas*

This paper describes the purchase of a shirt made by Juan Navarro on September 24, 1964. Juan is a goat-herder who lives in a narrow mountain valley in northeastern Mexico. I met him and the other men mentioned in this paper during the fall of 1963. Two graduate students and I were excavating a rock shelter near Juan's home, and for almost four months we lived in a tent close by the site. Juan and his friends were employed as our laborers. I returned to the same site in the fall of 1964 to continue excavations, and, in the process, gathered the information reported on here.

About 120 kilometers (75 miles) southeast of Monterrey is the town of Linares, Nuevo Leon. Its 18,000 inhabitants make it the second largest city in the state, and it is one of the oldest in northeastern Mexico. Linares has two hotels, between twenty and thirty clothing stores, two movie houses, five gas stations, mechanics, bakeries, a bus station, and paved streets. Except for the three motels along the old Monterrey-Mexico highway which caters to tourists, most of the income of Linares derives from agriculture and the business caused by the demands of its own population.

In 1961 Linares was connected to the highlands of Mexico by a new highway that was cut through the Sierra Madre, and joined Linares with Iturbide and Galeana, and San Roberto, and ultimately, Saltillo, Torreon, and Mexico City. The highway is a vast improvement over the old road that followed the valley floor. The latter would wash out continually, and be virtually impassable during the rainy season. Today, it is possible to make the ascent from Linares to Iturbide in an hour, following a road that passes through mountains of breath-taking beauty. Formerly, a truck would take almost a day, and sometimes longer.

Now that the highway is here, trucks pass through it continually. They come from Mexico, Saltillo, Queretero, Matehuala, Eagle Pass (in Texas), and use the highway to go south to Ciudad Victoria or north to Monterrey. The town of Linares is the lowland terminus of the highway, and the truck drivers usually stop in town for gas and food before taking off again. Surprisingly, the new highway has brought only one new industry, a fruit-packing plant, to Linares. For the most part, the town is a way station. It is difficult to say how the road has affected the townspeople. It has certainly made Linares noisier, and has given those involved in vehicle repair and the sale of gasoline greater business, but as far as I could gather, the town has been changed only slightly. The major impact of the road seems to have been on the *campesinos* who live between Linares and Galeana. They now go into town more often, and more quickly. They are now connected to life in Linares in a way that they never were previously. For them Lopez Mateos was Mexico's greatest President, for the highway was constructed during his administration.

Like Monterrey, Linares is situated at the eastern edge of the towering Sierra Madre Oriental. As you follow the highway west from Linares, you go for about 25 kilometers before reaching the base of the mountain range. These 25 kilometers are largely alluvial flood plains formed by material emptied out of the narrow valley streams from the highlands. In the fall, the streams are full and the land is green. During the hot and very dry summers, most of the streams are dry. It is this flood plain land that is used for agriculture, for corn (called Maize in Mexico), beans, and occasionally wheat.

As soon as one enters the narrow valley that snakes into the Sierra Madre, the nature of the land changes. The flood plain is gone. Instead there are steep mountains often with slopes of 45 degrees. The only level spots in the whole valley are the occasional terraces formed by the stream in parts where the valley has widened. Living on one of these terraces, approximately 31 kilometers from Linares, are the families of Juan Navarro, Musio Rodriguez, Mariano Davila, and Isidro Bravo. Here the land is unsuited for farming, but it is possible to raise goats, pigs, and cattle, and this is the major economic pursuit of the four men mentioned above.

Juan, Musio, Mariano, and Isidro live relatively close together, at least in terms of life in the valley. All live on ejido (community-owned) land. Juan, Musio, and Mariano, whose houses are separated by a hundred yards, live on the western border of the Ejido Las Crucitas, which was formed in 1938. Isidro, whose home is about one kilometer upstream, lives on the eastern border of the Ejido Santa Rosa. The latter is newly formed, having been privately owned land up until 1960. Although they live technically on different ejidos, the four men are essentially neighbors. They work together, are compadres to one another, and live a life that is outwardly very much alike. But, they differ from one another in many ways. Although the main object of this paper is Juan Navarro, a brief sketch of all four men is well worthwhile.

By far the most ambitious man is Musio Rodriguez. Musio is fifty-five years old, and the wealthiest of the four. In addition to his home in the valley, he also has a small ranch close to the pueblo of Las Crucitas, which he farms. Besides this he has a one-room house in the west end of Linares. Musio has two sons and two daughters. All of his children have been or are presently in school. His oldest son, Rogelio, is now twenty years old, and Musio was able to send him to commercial school for two years where he learned accounting, and, as Musio proudly says, learned how to use a typewriter. After Rogelio's schooling was completed, his father bought him a store at the western end of Linares, on the main street that connects to the highway. Here Rogelio sells foodstuffs and assorted groceries.

Musio is often a difficult man to find, for if he is not in town, he is either working the ranch, or herding his goats in the valley, or drumming up some other kind of work. He is constantly on the go, looking for a way of earning extra money. Musio has been in the states a number of times, having spent almost a whole year working in the Rio Grande Valley, near McAllen, Texas. He knows how to operate a tractor, and drive a truck. During the construction of the highway, Musio worked as a foreman. He has also worked in the lumber mills that are on top of the mountains near by. While we were digging here in the fall of 1963, and when my students were here alone in the summer of the same year, Musio was the man upon which they leaned. He is unquestionably a leader, a man who knows how to get things done, a man who does things well. Yet in spite of his accomplishments, and his year in the states, Musio apparently knows no English.

Juan Navarro has ambition, but unlike Musio, is not able to realize his desires. He is thirty-one years old, married for seven years, and has four children. He can read and write, and gives the general impression of being a quiet "scholarly" sort of fellow. Juan is certainly the most curious of the four in regard to inquiring about the world outside of Linares. He reads the newspapers, which the others apparently do not, and it is Juan rather than Musio who speaks about the importance of education. Juan wants to know about communism and how it is different from Democracy, and he is not at all clear on the subject. How much Juan understands of the current world scene, I do not know, but at least he asks questions.

Given this intellectual curiosity, interest in education, and especially his oft-stated views that his children must have an education, Juan's move to this valley three years ago seems somewhat difficult to understand. His two oldest children are old enough to be admitted to the second and third grade, but since they live in the valley where there is no school bus to take them to Las Crucitas, they cannot get an education. Juan could go back to Las Crucitas, where he was born and raised, but he says he is happier here in the valley, where he can be a shepherd most of the time. Juan's ambition is not so much to leave the valley as it is to leave Mexico. He wants to move to the states (he refers to it as "the other side") where there is real opportunity, and where his children can get a good education. He has a good idea of what life on the other side is like for he has worked in Texas, Arizona, Arkansas, and Oklahoma harvesting cotton, and he thinks the United States is very beautiful. Yet, there seems to be little chance that Juan will ever get into the United States. He has no parents in the United States, he has no one who will write him a letter assuring employment, and he does not speak English.

Mariano Davila also arrived in the valley three years ago, having lived, like Juan, formerly in Las Crucitas. He has been married fourteen years, and has four children. Mariano is thirty-four years old. The last time he went to the states was 10 years ago, but prior to that he had made trips throughout the southwest as a harvest hand. He speaks no English, and doesn't seem to be especially anxious to go to the United States again. Before he came here to the valley, he raised cattle and goats, and farmed, he said, over 8 hectares of land (a hectare is 2.5 acres). But he does not like farming, because there is too much risk, and too much work. (Northeastern Mexico is so dry that many farmers in neighboring ejidos have not been able to harvest corn for three years in a row.) Mariano has worked on the road during its construction, and is able to operate air hammers, and use dynamite. He is a strong man who enjoys using his strength. When he worked for us, Mariano insisted on doing the hardest jobs of all; he took enormous delight in being able to pick longer, shovel harder, and carry more than the others.

For Mariano, the life in the valley is rough but better than that in the lowlands. He phrases it simply—he would rather earn most of his money through herding, rather than through farming. Like Juan, he has a child of school age, but fortunately, he is able to have his son go to school. This last is accomplished because Mariano has a parent living in the Ejido of Ojo de Agua, where a schoolteacher comes three afternoons a week, and so Mariano's son stays with his grandfather for half the week during the school year.

Isidro Bravo, as already noted, lives about a kilometer up the valley from Musio, Mariano, and Juan. He is forty years old, has been married over twenty years and has five children. He moved down to his present location about three years ago from the municipio of Iturbide. The main reasons for his move were all economic, for he figured that he could live just as well here and for less. He had lived previously on a hill where he had to pay a grazing fee for his stock. The fee was 12 centavos per goat per month, and 3 pesos per cow per year. There was no charge for putting up a house on the land. Isidro decided that since he had over one hundred head of goats and two cows, the fees were prohibitive, and he walked both his family and his herd down to their present location. There are perhaps other advantages to the move that Isidro did not list. He now lives closer to Linares where the prices of all commodities are cheaper, and where there is more to see.

Like the others, Isidro has worked on the other side on a number of occasions. He was in the states last, about three years ago, and he says that he would like to go again sometime. In general, Isidro gives the impression of being the most adjusted man in the group of four. He has no desire to move out of the valley, especially since he noted that he saves money by living here. One of the obvious difficulties about life in the valley is that his three school-age children cannot get an education. Isidro admits that had he stayed in Iturbide his children could now be in school, but then, he wouldn't be able to clothe them adequately because of the cost of living differences. The problem is not so much his, he has said, as that of the government. The trouble with the Mexican government he says, is that it doesn't care about the poor man.

The Economic Base

There is only one major source of income for the four men, and that is through herding. Each supplements this income by farming a few hectares of land in the lowlands, but this last is considered as uncertain returns. Any other activity, such as working for archaeologists, helping on road construction or in the lumber mills, is purely supplemental and quite rare. Musio is the only one of the four who can count on an extra-curricular income of this nature. Some idea of how difficult it is to gain employment in this area may be gained from the fact that neither Juan, Mariano, nor Isidro had obtained any other form of employment since I left them on December 15, 1963. Thus, for nine months, these men had to live off the produce they raised.

Herding in the valley is a relatively simple operation, that requires very little capital expenditures. Since the property is all ejido land, there is no grazing fee. The animals are not fed grain, and only rarely are certain plants actually cut for them as fodder. The only expense involved in feed is the occasional purchase of salt, which even in the eyes of Juan, is only a nominal cost. Most of the herding as such is done by the children whose job it is to lead or follow the goats from one pasture to another. These are high up the steep slopes, and the children who climb the thorn studded mountains barefoot are almost as agile as any of the goats in their flock. The size of the flocks vary with the seasons, and with the demands of those who purchase the animals. During the summers of 1963 and 1964, Juan told me he had close to 150 animals; whereas during the fall, he estimated he had about half that amount.

In addition to the goats, each man owns a couple of cows, and a number of pigs. These animals are not fed either. The pigs seem to be the best foragers of the lot. In the fall of 1963, we were able to follow the growth of four litters of pigs, each consisting of eight or nine animals. Surprisingly, even though each litter had one runty animal, and sometimes two, every pig survived. The pigs come from stock that is well known in the United States. I saw Duroc-Jerseys, Hampshires, and Poland-Chinas, all apparently of reasonably pure-bred stock. The cows were seldom seen, since they spent most of their time high up in the mountains. Of all the animals in the valley, the cattle seemed to be the least successful, and the most hybrid. They were of dairy rather than meat breeds, but I was unable to determine with which breed most of these animals were most closely affiliated.

Besides the goats, pigs, and cows, each family has a number of chickens that are kept for eggs and food.

For the most part selling the animals presents few problems, and these are now even less since the highway has come through. The terrace on which the men live is visible from the highway. Every few days dealers drive up and down the road offering to purchase animals. Goats are sold this way. A young animal (*cabrito*) usually sells for about 25 pesos, a mature female will bring about 85 pesos. The prices are reasonably stable, and the demand for goats is constant. Pigs and cattle, however, are not sold to the dealers on the road, for these are sold by weight, and the dealers seldom have scales. Usually pigs are sold in Linares, and the men often carry them into the bus when they go to town.

As noted earlier, each man supplements his income by some farming in the lowlands. All the men, except Musio, farm on ejido land exclusively, and usually work a plot with other members of their family, or sometimes, among friends. I am told that a man and his aids will be able to work 8 hectares of land with ease. In a good year, 8 hectares will produce about 10 tons of corn. Since a hectare is about 2.5 acres, this is a yield of only 18 bushels per acre. Such a harvest in the United States is terribly low, but here in the dry northeast of Mexico, where the farmers plant a small eared non-hybrid dent corn, such a yield is exceptional.

The men have little idea of how much money they earn in a year. They told me that they sold a cabrito about once a week, which at the rate of 25 pesos per animal, gave 1300 pesos per year. If this is doubled, to account for income gained through the sale of pigs, and farm produce, we have about 2600 pesos ($208) per annum. When I produced that figure, the men, after reflection, thought it might be a bit high, but was approximately correct. During the ten weeks that the men worked for us, they were getting paid at the almost exorbitant rate of 100 pesos per week, for a full six day week.[1] Thus, in 1963, they were able to supplement their annual income by a full 1000 pesos ($80) by working for archaeologists.

None of the men saved any money, either in a pot or in a bank. The general practice is to spend whatever funds are at hand within a few days after the money is received. When the men worked for us, they would usually go into town on payday (Saturdays) with their families, and spend it all that night. They would come back in the bus loaded with their purchases. Very often I would loan Juan money in advance, two or three days after payday. His case however was unusual at that time since most of his salary went towards the purchase of medicines for his child. I asked both Juan and Isidro how long after we had left in December, was the last of their salary spent. Both men told me that it was all gone within two days.

The income gained through the sale of an animal is also spent immediately, but there is a difference between funds obtained through wages and through the sale of livestock. The latter are sold when the money is needed. The wages we paid the men were viewed as extra income, and were used to purchase many of the things that, although badly needed, could still wait awhile if need be.

None of the men felt that a bank offered any advantage to them. Even Musio Rodriguez, the richest man of the group, has no bank account. If there may be said to be any kind of saving, it is that represented by the animal on the hoof; and its growth that costs nothing, is as good as ac-

---

[1] It should be noted that 100 pesos per week, while a good salary in the country, is not considered as such in Monterrey. There a good laborer, I have been told, often gets 20 pesos a day, and more.

cumulating interest. Since each man has a herd of goats that exceed, at this writing, one hundred animals apiece, their stock probably makes them wealthier than many families living in Linares.

Cost of and Standard of Living

One day, shortly before he made the purchase described in this paper, I asked Juan Navarro what were his major economic concerns. He answered very quickly, "food and clothes," he said. "How about housing?" I asked. "That is never a problem," he said, "for I can always make a house." In many ways, Juan's lack of concern for his shelter, and his worry about food and clothing, reflects a dominant attitude of most of the people in northeastern Mexico.

Throughout much of Mexico, a house is a one-room structure. The average dimensions run perhaps about 15 feet wide, and 25 to 35 feet in length. There is a door, and occasionally a window. The major variations on this plan are largely in regard to size and the kinds of material used in house construction. These, to a great extent, depend upon the local culture patterns and what materials are available for building. In Iturbide, for example, where there is little soil, stone-walled houses are the rule, and the roofs are usually made of wood shingles. In Linares, most of the houses are either of adobe or wattle and daub (laced sticks bound together by mud). Occasional houses are made of cement block. But whether one lives in Iturbide or Linares, most of the floors are of dirt, and the sewage facilities are of the most primitive kind.

As one leaves Linares to go into the highlands, the houses become increasingly primitive. The most striking feature of the houses in Las Crucitas and those in the neighboring ranches is that they are largely made of sticks or boards with no chinking or daubing. While such a dwelling may be delightfully airy during the hot summers, it is most uncomfortable during the winter when the night temperatures are often in the low twenties.

The houses of Juan, Musio, and Mariano are all made of hand-hewn boards, and the roofs are of thatch. Isidro's house is made of brush and also has a thatched roof. The men all agree that one man working alone, that is with just the help of his immediate family, can make such a house within a week. Apparently this estimate is reasonably accurate, for a similar period was offered by others living closer to Linares.

Furniture in the houses of the four men is almost nonexistent. Once, when I asked them if they made their own furniture, they laughed. "What furniture?" they asked. The families use no beds. In the summer and during the warmer months of the year, everyone sleeps on mats lying on the ground. During the colder months, they use mattresses, made of burlap bags stuffed with tree moss. For chairs almost everyone uses stumps of wood to sit on, and, since they hold the food bowl in their laps, there is no need for a table. Juan, in this respect, is exceptional since he has a chair. This last is one of two remaining from the time he was married seven years ago. The chair is of local manufacture, and cost 7 pesos new. It is now virtually unusable. The major item of furniture, if it may be called that, is a box or valise that is used to store the family's clothes. Hangers are not used. The second most important furniture item is a 2-peso, kerosene lamp.

For Musio, Juan and the others, a house is not a prestige symbol but simply a place to sleep, a place to keep dry in, a place for family privacy, and a place in which to store things. It is not a place in which to *live,* as the word is so meaningfully used in the United States. Yet, this attitude towards house and furnishings seems extreme. I have seen better made dwellings both in the highlands and the lowlands close by, houses that show the extra care that pride gives. Many have beds, chairs, tables, potted plants outside, and various forms of decoration. These touches do not occur among our four families. For them, the major demonstration of pride that would be familiar to an American, is to be found in their clothing. When they go to town, or to a fiesta in the ejido, they are then well dressed.

It seems difficult to overestimate the importance of clothing. A clean set of clothes is for a pass into town, or a fiesta. Clothes are the mark of a man's self-respect, and the ability of a man to clothe his family is in many ways the measure of a man. I once asked Mariano in the presence of Isidro and Juan why he wanted the new pair of trousers he had just purchased, when the pair he was wearing in the field seemed perfectly acceptable. He told me that while they were acceptable for the field, they could not be worn into town, for they were much too shabby. "They would call me a hick," he said, "if they saw me go into town this way." "Who?" I asked. "Why, everyone," he answered, adding some delightful obscenities to punctuate his feelings. Isidro thought my questions hysterically funny, for everyone knows what it is like to go into town without a good set of clothes. "Oh they would laugh; they would call him many funny things; they would call him————. They would call anyone these things if they came into town badly dressed." If the clothes are clean, and not threadbare, they are acceptable. Once they begin to frazzle, they are then relegated to work clothes.

Juan, like the others has essentially three sets of clothes for himself. These consist of one pair for going into town, one reasonably good pair of field clothes, which had just recently been used for dress wear, and finally one pair of work clothes that were almost threadbare. The "outfit" consists of a pair of cotton trousers, a shirt, undershorts, and a sombrero. He estimates that the three shirts he buys every year cost him about 50 pesos apiece, that the trousers cost about the same, and the undershorts are close to 10 pesos a pair. The sombreros worn in this country are of straw, and Juan estimated that he used between two and three a year. They cost him about 20 pesos each. When Juan is working in the field he wears the typical leather sandals of this region, which consist of a flattened tire segment for a sole, that is tied to the foot with a loose lacing. The sandals cost between 12 and 15 pesos a pair, and will usually go for three months without needing repairs. One pair of sandals will last for almost two years if properly taken care of. But while sandals are perfectly acceptable in the field, neither Juan nor the others would wear sandals in town. For this, shoes and socks must be worn. Juan has a pair of shoes that he bought three years ago, at 80 pesos a pair. The socks that go with the shoes do not nearly wear as well, and Juan has to buy about one pair a year.

Juan estimated that this year he will probably have to spend about 1000 pesos on clothing for himself and his family. The big items this year will be warm jackets for the whole family, and possibly some sweaters. He noted that last winter was mighty cold, and it looked as if the coming winter would be more severe than usual. Since they use no fire in the house, either for cooking or for heating, the jackets were necessary to keep warm in at night as one slept, and also for the cooler parts of the morning and evening. Juan also noted that he needed a shirt very badly. He had discussed this with his wife about a month before the purchase (described in this paper) was made. It was decided that a shirt was probably more necessary than a jacket, and, when the time came to buy one, it would get first priority.

The Stores

Most of the purchases made by Juan and his friends are made in Linares, because the prices there are cheaper than those in Iturbide. The latter is a smaller town, with less stores, and cannot offer as wide a selection as the stores in Linares. Furthermore, even though now connected to the lowlands by the new highway, Iturbide is still relatively isolated, and out of the way, and most items are more expensive than elsewhere. In point of fact, the only person who regularly goes to Iturbide for purchases is Isidro, and this is primarily because he has an uncle who runs a store there. The uncle, who sells clothing, allows Isidro to pay for his purchases slowly, and for Isidro this is a blessing.

While the men were employed by us, during the fall of 1963, we had the impression that they did most of their shopping in the grocery of Rogelio Rodriguez. I asked them if the prices were lower in Rogelio's store than in the others, and, since Rogelio's father Musio is part of the group discussed here, I naturally expected an affirmative answer. Juan, Mariano, and Isidro, however, were very definite in their answer. "No, Rogelio's prices are higher." They bought food and other items from Rogelio only when they had limited funds and could afford to make only small purchases. Rogelio would cut up a bar of soap, or split a package of lard, and sell each portion for more. They realized that they were paying more for these services; they also stated that when more money was on hand, they would not buy from him.

The men have definite opinions about shopping and shops in town. All of them asserted that they look around for the lowest possible price on all commodities before making any purchase. They also noted that the stores in the center of town, which were owned by the Lebanese (called arabes) were unnecessarily expensive and consequently they never shopped there. Although no man knew exactly where his neighbor shopped, all had the impression that their friends went to the smaller stores close to the center, but not in it. Each man said he had a store that he liked more than the others, but, for the most part, where they ultimately made a purchase, it was for price alone.

The Purchase

On Friday, September 24, I paid the men their week's wages. It was almost dark when we got through working and had just started to rain. Although it was much too late and miserable to go into town, I had to spend the weekend in Monterrey. I told the men that I would be going in, and automatically offered anyone a lift if they wanted it. Juan asked for a ride in spite of the late hour, though I could not offer him a return trip. He hurried on to change his clothes, and I waited for him at the truck.

He met me about fifteen minutes later wearing his going-to-town clothes—a pretty frayed and slightly soiled white shirt, a pair of sun-tan trousers (with cuffs) that had been bleached almost white by laundering, a pair of worn unpolished black shoes, green cotton socks, and a reasonably clean straw hat.

After the truck started moving, Juan mentioned that he had decided to buy the shirt today. There was going to be a wedding in Ojo de Agua tomorrow he said, and, after touching his shirt, he noted that he couldn't go in the one he was wearing. He also said that he would try to pick up a dress for his eight-year-old daughter. Usually the women buy children's clothing, but since his wife was not going to town with him, she asked him to buy the dress too.

I asked Juan where he was going to go shopping, and whether or not he intended to buy anything in the center of town. He answered negatively. No, he would not buy anything in the arabes' stores in the center because they were much too expensive. He said that he would look around to see what was available. He had a few favorite stores, and he would give them a try first.

I parked the truck close to the main plaza in Linares and followed Juan. He walked past the arabes' stores in the center without looking in the windows, and went at once to a dry goods shop located about five blocks away.

The shop was located at the corner of the block. It consisted of a single room, about 35 feet long and 25 feet wide, with a very high ceiling. There was a front and side door, but no windows. The walls were lined with shelves, and down the middle of the store ran a long counter, at one end of which was a small glass display case. The wall behind the counter was crammed from floor to ceiling with shoes, hats, folded dresses, and bolts of cheap cotton and cotton-rayon printed fabrics. One of the side walls was devoted largely to cheap jackets made of cotton and black leather. Here was also a canvas cot with an aluminum frame. The glass case held some pretty combs and three pairs of women's shoes. The wall in front of the counter held men's clothing—work shirts and trousers of blue denim, others of sun-tan cotton twill. One part of the wall was also devoted to a display of men's shirts, all of which were wrapped in pliofilm bags. Other shirts were boxed and in shelves against the same wall. Between the boxes of shirts, and the work clothes was a small dressing room, about 5 feet high and less than 2 feet square. It was a make-shift affair, outlined with a few boards, and covered with trousers on hangers, but it gave some privacy.

As we walked in the shop, Juan told me that he often made purchases here, and that it was his favorite shop. If the owner recognized Juan, he certainly did not show it; he greeted us with the customary *Buenos Tardes,* and then said, "Tell me what you want." The store was empty at the time, except for ourselves, the owner, and his girl assistant. She stayed near the entrance throughout the time Juan and I spoke to the owner. She busied herself folding dresses, and underwear.

Juan told the owner that he was thinking about buying a shirt. In response to the shopkeeper's query, he told him that he wore a 14½. The owner went to the wall rack and took down about six shirts, of various colors and designs, all wrapped in pliofilm bags. Juan picked up each shirt and carefully examined it in the semidarkness of the shop. He ran the pliofilm bag tightly between his fingers as if he could feel the quality of the fabric inside. He kept coming back to one shirt, a dark green one made by Medalla that matched his socks, but since the size was 15, a half size larger than his own, he felt concerned. The owner went to the front of the counter and started opening boxes of shirts in Juan's size, but found nothing that Juan found satisfactory. Finally, the shopkeeper suggested that possibly Juan was mistaken about his size, and so, as Juan bent his head forward, the owner leaned over the counter, and examined Juan's shirt collar. The size marking had long since washed away, but the shopkeeper at least was able to observe that Juan was wearing a Clover shirt. (This brand, as well as Medalla, are comparable to Arrow and Manhattan in the United States.) Finally, almost in desperation, Juan decided to take the dark green shirt he had originally chosen. He asked the price and was told 42 pesos. Juan looked at the shirt a moment, and then offered 40 pesos. The price was accepted. Juan then asked to try on the shirt, for size, and the shopkeeper acquiesced. He took the shirt carefully from the pliofilm bag, removed the pins, cardboard backing, and tissue lining, and gave the shirt to Juan. Juan went back to the dressing room, put the shirt on, and came out with the shirt hanging outside his trousers. He did not have the neck buttoned, since he never wears a tie, and so his concern about the half-size difference seemed groundless. Juan finally announced that the shirt fitted, without asking either of our opinions, and went back to the dressing room. He came out wearing his old white shirt, and gave the green one to the shopkeeper to rewrap. The shirt was carefully folded with its tissue paper, and cardboard backing put in place, pinned, and then placed once again in the pliofilm bag. The packing was done with the skill of a man with many years of practice. The shopkeeper finally took the shirt, wrapped it in a newspaper, and gave it to Juan. Juan presented two 20-peso bills, and we walked out of the store together.

Juan returned with me to the truck. As we started back, we once again passed the windows of the Lebanese shops in the center of town. Juan decided to look in the window this time, and almost instantly spotted a shirt identical to the one just purchased. The price tag read 40 pesos, which was what Juan had bargained for. Other shirts of the same brand, but with short sleeves, were offered at 32 pesos. Juan was visibly shocked. The prices of shirts in "the most expensive store in town" were obviously less than the store he considered his favorite. As I drove away in the truck, I could see that Juan still had a worried expression in his face. He looked very much like a man who knows he has been cheated.

Summary

Juan Navarro lives in a world where a good appearance, as indicated by a clean unraveled set of clothes, is a necessary requisite for going to town or attending a fiesta. In order to participate in this culture, he must buy about three sets of clothes for himself each year.

Like most of us, Juan feels compelled to say that he minds his pennies, that he looks for the best price, that he bargains for whatever is purchased. His actions, however, reveal that he does not always shop around, and that he is not particularly adept at bargaining. When something appeals to him strongly, as did the shirt he bought, the rules of frugality are apt to be disregarded. He could have gone to another store to find a shirt exactly his size, but he did not. He could have bought a less expensive brand, but he did not. He could have offered 38 pesos instead of 40 pesos, but he did not want to jeopardize his bargaining position and make the shirt unobtainable.

One of the axioms of Juan's culture is that the stores of the Lebanese in the center of town are more expensive, and so he felt no necessity in examining their prices before he made his purchases in his "favorite" shop. His discovery, that the identical shirt could have been bought from the Lebanese for the same price, and, if he had bargained, possibly even less, shocked him visibly. Like the poor of many areas, Juan Navarro deals with shops that cater to the poor. In so doing, he often spends more for a given item than those who are wealthier than he.

6 / Introduction to THE WRONG STATUS SYMBOL

Moving to a new city, Mrs. Superscript, a middle-aged matron, discovered that she had an entré to a lower-upper-class group through a former childhood acquaintance. Being forced to purchase a car, and being financially middle-class, she selected a used, gold Cadillac—an action inconsistent with either her present or former place in society.

Of all the cases in this book, Parsons' is the clearest case of direct social influence in which the object purchased is chosen almost entirely on the basis of the impression it will make on a particular group of people. The choice of an inappropriate automobile can be explained in part by the obvious anxiety of Mrs. Superscript; it is well known that choices made under anxiety are likely to be ineffective.

But there is at least one other way in which to analyze the events described. Mrs. Superscript is clearly at a major choice point in her life, one that is characterized by profound emotional involvement. Like most fringe members of a group, she undoubtedly feels that she must conform more closely to group norms than other members. But when one assesses the quality of her action, he sees that she has behaved in a way that essentially flaunts the standards of the group and proclaims the most florid aspects of her own individuality.

Despite emotional pressures, this seems an unlikely turn of events in a decision made by an intelligent woman. For this reason, it makes considerable sense to regard the purchase of the used, gold Cadillac as a direct first step in withdrawal from the group. Membership in the group costs more than she can afford, includes such unenjoyable activities as bridge, makes her repress a natural exuberance, and is beginning to generate problems at home. It seems quite probable that she recognizes her own discomfort in the new situations at least subconsciously.

Such an analysis suggests that the purchase, while largely subconscious, accurately stated her relationship to the groups involved. It told her family that she was not going to continue as a fringe member of the

81

social group. It stated to the group that her values were different from theirs; and it probably served as a symbol for Mrs. Superscript herself, bringing her subconscious feelings closer to the level of consciousness.

THE WRONG STATUS SYMBOL
Wilbur Banks Parsons

My sister, whom I shall call Mrs. Deborah Superscript, recently made a purchase of a three-year-old Cadillac Sedan de Ville. Her son, her husband, and I regarded the act as one of the least characteristic we could remember.

Debbie is an outgoing woman, practical and spirited. She lives life, or seems to, on an active, day-to-day basis. In this she is somewhat like our father, who might be described as a plunger. He was an entrepreneur who was constantly putting the family money into some new venture that promised fabulous success. A number of his investments were quite successful, at least for a time, but they were always followed by ones that failed. Neither the successes nor the failures could teach him caution or dampen his enthusiasm for the next long shot.

Mother came from one of the "good" families of the southeast, although not one of the wealthy ones. It is possible that she put up more front than necessary when one of Dad's ventures was collapsing. With the many moves, up or down in a given town's social structure, away to a new city in a new state, she had a difficult time letting us know our position in society. A statement that might seem pretentious at one moment appeared modest only a few months later.

Perhaps the depression was particularly difficult for people of both the age and the entrepreneurial character of my father. Although I got through college before the bottom in 1932, Debbie had to withdraw after her freshman year and take a job as secretary. Some of Debbie's essential personality is shown in her periodic enrollment and ultimate graduation from college after eight years. By that time she was married. Her husband, a mechanical engineer, was quite different from our father. He moved a great deal, even changed jobs, but the direction was steadily upward. And, if the progress was not meteoric, neither was it slow. When the corporation for which he worked transferred him to head the Atlanta operation, his responsibilities and salary were above those he had anticipated even a few years earlier.

Debbie and her husband rented a house after the move because they were new to the city and wanted to be sure that they built or bought in the right area. Then Debbie met an old friend she had known in childhood. The woman had married a prominent Atlanta lawyer, a director in several corporations. Debbie was not only delighted to find a friend but was impressed by the social standing of someone she regarded to be no better than herself. It would be a mistake to overstate the social position of Debbie's friend. She was not a member of one of the leading families in status or wealth, although her husband's income was probably two or three times as great as that of Debbie's husband. In effect, the attorney and his wife were in the lower-upper class, members of upper-class clubs and societies without really being among the power elite. A group of about thirty families clustered around the attorney's wife; and, almost before she realized it, Debbie was caught up in a group unlike any with which she had previously associated on a long-term basis. The houses of members were among the larger and older homes of that part of the city, selling for $50,000 to $150,000. They gathered daily in one of the group's homes for afternoon bridge or simply to talk. And country club get-togethers occurred at least once a week. Most of the group drove Cadillacs; a few employed chauffeurs. The richest member of the group drove an old Ford sedan and was noted for this eccentricity. Three members of the group were no longer wealthy enough to qualify but were tolerated since they were the descendants of major investors in one of the local companies. While entry to the group was difficult, Debbie was accepted because of the secure position of the attorney's wife, who vouched for her and proposed the Superscripts for the appropriate golf club.

Debbie's husband was what might be described as middle management in his organization. But as head of the Atlanta operation he was in a powerful position to make recommendations on purchases and construction. Several wealthy contractors entertained the family in hopes of future contracts.

Despite such auspicious beginnings in the new city, neither Debbie nor her husband could easily keep up with the social group of which the attorney's wife was a member. Entertainment expenses were high, and a fair amount of leisure was presumed. It was at this point that Debbie's son returned from college with the insistence of an eighteen-year-old that he needed a car. His mother had already felt the inadequacies of her Oldsmobile and let him have it rather than purchasing him a less expensive automobile. This left her with the dilemma of locating a machine for herself. Whatever her expectations, her husband made it clear that there was no possibility of their purchasing a new Cadillac at $6000. His interpretation of their finances was that a $4000 car would be stretching the family budget.

Neither wealthy enough to be able to indulge in a Ford of any vintage nor imaginative and secure enough to select a foreign sports car, Debbie began to shop for a Buick, Oldsmobile or Mercury. While looking she found a used Cadillac Sedan de Ville for about $3000. The gold and white car was easily within her price range, but it was clearly the wrong status symbol. At least the matter was clear to everyone but Debbie.

Debbie apparently viewed herself as a completely suitable member of the group in which she was moving. Although her most recent situation in another state had been a cut below it, so had her husband's job been less important than it now was. She easily identified with the lawyer's wife and certainly did not feel inferior, in any usual sense, to the women with whom she played bridge daily. Yet she was well aware of the costs involved—both time, money, and prescribed activity. She recognized that she would have to entertain frequently, assume duties in the Red Cross and the Art Association, join other appropriate clubs besides the golf club. For a while she had toyed with the idea of joining the Episcopal church rather than the Methodist church in which she had been raised. Already she had rejoined the Democratic party after a lengthy sojourn as a Republican in an area where that affiliation was more suitable.

Her perception of the Cadillac in relation to the group was less clear for a simple reason. If she had moved to Atlanta owning the same car, it would have been a point in her favor. If she had purchased it, used, just two or three days before running into the attorney's wife, it would have been a minor symbol legitimizing her aspirations. Anything she purchased within the price limits imposed upon her would, as she saw it, be something of a liability. It was simply not possible for her to see how much more of a liability the used, gold Cadillac might be.

I viewed, and I believe Debbie's husband viewed, their situation in quite different terms than she did. I regarded them as upper-middle class. Her husband's salary of $22,000 simply would not stretch to meet the demands of the lower-upper class group—especially the demands it would place upon its novitiates. And I doubted that Debbie had an independent interest in the group's activities. She merely tolerates bridge and is certainly not attracted to art associations or charitable organizations. She actively disliked several members of the group. But she has always been interested in the material standards that are a concomitant of wealth. She had occasional opportunities to taste them during the periodic successes of our father, and there was little chance for that taste to cloy. In fact, she had expressed before her Atlanta residence the desire for a Cadillac.

The days leading up to the purchase were difficult ones for Debbie, for her husband and son, and for me. All of us except my sister were opposed to the purchase; I was violently opposed. We attempted to reason with her and, in the process, found ourselves involved in endless arguments and recriminations that covered almost every element of the Superscript's life. I openly and heatedly doubted Debbie's rationality a number of times. Her son attacked the idea of the purchase and was implicitly accused of being the spendthrift who had made the purchase necessary. There were unpleasant moments when Debbie accused her husband of holding her back in her plans to entertain the group as frequently as she considered proper.

Knowing that Debbie was as strong a segregationist as southerners of our age are likely to be, I referred to the used, gold-and-white Cadillac as a "nigger's car" and "that nigger's cast-off car" often enough to convince myself that it probably was. Such purely emotional argument made her, if anything, more adamant, even as she was forced to admit the possibility of its former ownership. Intellectually, she understood all of the arguments, and has since said, "I knew they would look down on me if I bought a used Cadillac instead of a new, lower-priced car, and I thought about it a long time."

In the process she said that she didn't want to be rich, that all she wanted was to have what "they" had. She did not refer to the group as "we" or "us," clearly indicating that she was still an outsider, or that her membership in the group was, at best, marginal. She even talked with the lawyer's wife about the purchase and was told that the ownership of a prestige car was immaterial to the group. The elderly Ford of the wealthiest member was mentioned as an example of the group's disinterest in worldly goods. Debbie was not fooled. The lawyer's wife drove a Cadillac.

Debbie bought the car. It stopped running the second day she owned it and gave her trouble as long as it was in her possession.

For a total of about two years Debbie was a quasi-member of the group, entertaining less often than the principal members even after the Superscripts built a luxury home in a "good" neighborhood. In fact, the purchase of the home made it financially more difficult to continue to meet group expectations and surely impressed none of the members.

At the end of that time, the lawyer moved to Washington to take a government job, and Debbie was promptly dropped from the group. To maintain her marginal membership she needed not the right car, but the right friend in residence.

The consequenes of losing her temporary position in society have all been fortunate. Released from the nervous strain, Debbie has become more pleasant to members of her family, and obviously happier. She drives a new Buick and puts some of her considerable energy to work selling real estate. Her friends are of the upper middle class, people with whom both she and her husband feel comfortable. She still yearns to travel and to buy "things" and has more money with which to do so. The purchase of the Cadillac may actually have been instrumental in a minor way in her achievement of the present balance.

When asked about the purchase of the Cadillac, she remembers a blue, four-door sedan (also a used Cadillac) that was $300 cheaper. Then she says that, knowing what she knows now, she would make the same decision again.

7 / Introduction to PURCHASING AND LIVING WITH A SWIMMING POOL

Chauncey Vincent, an engineer working for the government in New Mexico, received a raise. This became the occasion for him and his family to purchase a swimming pool. The case concerns the kind of pool he purchased, the circumstances of the purchase, and the problems he encountered in the process.

While there are a number of aspects of consumer behavior to discuss in connection with the Vincents' purchase of a swimming pool, their income level and response to a pay raise suggest that their case is appropriate ground for the consideration of the function of marketing in a high-level economy. First, some have feared that as incomes increase, consumers will spend a lower percent of their income and that an increasing gap between income and expenditures will lead to economic stagnation. Second, Galbraith's insistence that affluence leads to an improper allocation of resources when present proportions of income are left in the hands of private persons for their own disposal has persuaded numbers of people to his point of view.

The Vincents are an excellent case in point. The pay raise they received placed them in the top 6.2 percent of families with regard to income. In effect, they had been preparing for this eventuality for at least a year. During the first year of the increase they spent not the total amount of the increase for that year, but what must have been at least twice the amount of the increase, and quite probably more. Making the ridiculous assumption that the Vincents are typical of all families with the same income or less, we arrive at a proposition: *the propensity to consume increases more rapidly than income increases.* Of course, no one really knows what increases in the family income do indicate because there is no adequate theory of consumer behavior based or empirical evidence.

Second, look at the social consequences of the purchase. The Vincents have taken some of the pressure off of public and other swimming pools making them slightly more desirable to swim in than previously because the Vincents and some of their friends are no longer adding to the crowd.

In other words, at some levels of income private expenditures may tend to supplement public expenditures rather than increase the need for them.

Obviously, both of the above generalizations relate to the function of marketing in society since it is likely that both the levels of demand and the particular goods and services desired are at least partially a result of marketing efforts.

A more adequate understanding of consumer behavior would undoubtedly improve the quality of economic analysis which now rests on rather gross and probably inaccurate notions about consumer expenditures. And it should suggest the extent to which individual choices may improve the quality of community life.

PURCHASING AND LIVING WITH A SWIMMING POOL

David Hamilton, *Department of Economics, The University of New Mexico*

Thirty years ago new private-home swimming pools were almost exclusively a symbol of very recent and large success. Hollywood stars were interviewed at the poolside and even Al Capone, whose success was a direct product of Prohibition, was featured beside a private swimming pool in Florida. Certainly the very rich had possessed private swimming pools before the advent of Hollywood and Prohibition. But these were the almost exclusive property of the residents of Newport and similar gathering places of those who seemed born to wealth rather than having recently come by it. The very rich did not disport themselves at poolside for the edification of a public following. Mrs. Astor's poolside antics, if any, were never prominently featured on the society pages. It is noteworthy that in their account of life in Muncie, Indiana, in the mid-twenties the Lynds make no mention of private swimming pools.[1] While failure to mention such a phenomenon cannot be taken as evidence of its nonexistence, it would seem to indicate that the swimming pool had not yet touched the Muncie upper middle class "way of life."

Today in Albuquerque, New Mexico, it is estimated that between 300

---

[1] Robert and Helen Lynd, *Middletown*. New York: Harcourt, 1929.

and 400 private pools are in use. This would seem to be on the conservative side, for the city population in 1963 was approximately 230,000 and the number of pools for which building permits were taken out in 1963 alone was sixty-four. Not all of these permits, however, were for private-home pools. One was for the new Elks Club and some were apparently for motels and similar semi-public use. The city building inspector's records do not always make a clear distinction possible. But assuming that of the sixty-four permits at least fifty were private-home pools and assuming that pool building proceeded in the four-year stretch, 1960 through 1963, at this pace the number of pools was probably at least 300. This would allow for only 100 pools in all the preceding years. This may seem unusually low, but it must be remembered that the flurry of home-pool building in Albuquerque began only about seven years ago when a few specialized firms entered the local market.

But whatever the number of home pools in existence that of Vincent's is one of these. The Vincent family is composed of six members, Chauncey and Ellen, husband and wife, and four children, Carol Ellen, Benny, John, and Crane. In 1960, when their pool was constructed, Carol Ellen was twelve, Benny was ten, John was seven, and Crane was four. The family moved to Albuquerque in 1958 from Washington, D.C. Chauncey, a chemist with the Atomic Energy Commission, has now been with the Albuquerque office six years.

Swimming is a recreation in which all of the Vincents participate. Chauncey was raised in Conneaut, Ohio, a summer recreation spot on the Lake Erie shore. Ellen is an excellent swimmer. At the time the decision was made to purchase the pool Carol Ellen and Benny were members of the Acapulco Swimming Club Team. Ellen helped coach the team. All have continued to swim both competitively as well as merely for recreation.

When living in Washington, D.C., the Vincents were members of a community pool, a part of the development in which they lived. They did not consider starting a community or cooperative pool in Albuquerque as they did not move into a new development. Their home is in an old neighborhood as neighborhoods are dated in Albuquerque, a rapidly growing western city, the area having been built up approximately ten years before they moved into it.

In Albuquerque they did have access to large swimming pools, one of which is on Sandia Base, an interservice military installation in Albuquerque. On the Base is Coronado pool, which is an adjunct of the civilian employees club to which employees of AEC have access. They felt that both of these arrangements were less desirable than a pool at their own home. Coronado pool was approximately three miles from their home and

Acapulco was about one mile. The distance was probably less objectionable than getting six individuals back and forth from the pool. A minor objection was Ellen's preference for two piece bathing suits for swimming combined with her objection to the wearing of such suits in public.

They also considered joining a country club in Albuquerque in order to have use of the pool. But Chauncey and Ellen state this was rejected despite the fact Chauncey is a golf player with the comment, "We are not the country-club type." Chauncey now plays golf on a course operated by the University of New Mexico and on a public course belonging to the City of Albuquerque.

The family considered constructing a pool on a do-it-yourself basis. Chauncey has better than average skills in home maintenance. Some pools in Albuquerque have been constructed by the owners; even more home modification and addition is done in the city by the do-it-yourself route. Most of the homes in Albuquerque are one story and easily lend themselves to addition. In fact, in the older Spanish culture it was once the custom to construct the houses of adobe. Rooms were simply added to accommodate augmentations of the family. The house grew as the family grew. Today relatively few homes are of adobe, but the one-story construction has continued as well as the practice of adding on to accommodate an expanded family; it was a common practice. The previous owner of Vincent's home made some additions; Vincent, however, did no more than give it casual consideration.

The decision to hire a contractor and to go ahead with the pool was made in 1960. The immediate catalytic agent was a sizable across-the-board Federal pay increase that year. The pay increase put a pool within reach of the Vincent's budget, although they had been considering such a venture for at least a year. Once the decision was made to purchase a pool they did some research on pools. This, however, was not exhaustive. They did not go to *Consumer Reports* of Consumer Union or *Consumer Bulletin* of Consumers Research. *Consumer Reports* published a rather extensive article on the home swimming pool in its March 1960 issue and Consumer Bulletin had several articles in 1957 and 1958.[2] But they did some research at the public library and visited one other family who had a liner-type pool. The latter visit, however, was not made until they had themselves decided on a liner-type pool. Since the family they visited was satisfied with theirs,

[2] "Swimming Pools: Construction, Maintenance, and Financing Problems Can Easily Get You In Over Your Head," *Consumer Reports*, vol. 25, 3, March 1960, pp. 134-139; "The Facts on Swimming Pools," *Consumer Bulletin*, vol. 41, 6, June 1958; "The Facts on Swimming Pools II," *Consumer Bulletin*, vol. 41, 7, July 1958; "Dangers from Swimming Pool Pumps," *Consumer Bulletin*, vol. 39, 6, June 1957.

this bit of "research" had the effect of confirming the "wisdom" of their decision.

Some individuals claim that they are deterred from having a pool because of the public responsibility. One hears of the pool as a menace to wandering small children. About a decade ago one family in Albuquerque had a neighbor's child drown in their pool; and although public liability insurance can be secured, the specter of such a tragedy is reason enough for some people to refrain from having a pool though it falls within their budget. The Vincents did consider this, but felt that this danger was overstated. They felt that the danger of hitting a child with an automobile was much greater than that of a child drowning in a home pool, and yet we do all drive automobiles. They also felt that they could control this hazard and that their neighborhood was not one with very many small, nonswimming children. One other reason often given for not putting in a pool by individuals who might otherwise do so is the effect of a pool on the resale value of the house. Some contend that the resale value may be lowered and others contend that, while not lowered, the appreciation in the value of the house is not equal to the cost of the pool. The Vincents did not give this much consideration as they looked upon the house as a place in which to live rather than as an investment with resale value. They did not consult with anyone on this point. It should be emphasized that Chauncey is a professional person and has little or no experience in the business or commercial world. He was once employed by a commercial drug firm, but as a chemist in the research division. He does not assess every family activity in terms of its investment value. The Bernalillo County assessor claims that pools do increase the value of a house in the Albuquerque area, but limit the number of potential buyers if it is necessary to sell. Those who are in the market for a house with a pool are willing to pay more.

When the Vincents entered the market for a pool in the summer of 1960, ten firms were listed in the yellow pages of the Bernalillo County telephone directory as Swimming Pool Contractors and Dealers. The number dwindled to seven in 1964, only two of which had been in operation in 1960. The rash of home-pool construction firms, that lasted for about three years in the late 1950s is apparently now over and the business is stabilized in the Albuquerque area. But even though there is enough pool construction to afford several firms fairly steady business, it is still one with a high turnover and with several firms building only occasionally. When interviewed, one of the existent firms claimed that they built about thirty pools a year. This appeared to be the most flourishing one. If their claim was true, however, they must have included construction outside Bernalillo County because city building permits do not substantiate such a business.

The builders of pools sometimes are general contractors who also engage in patios, blockwalls, and home additions. Some of them operate a pool construction firm under a name differing from that of the parent construction firm. This is perhaps because of the specialized nature of pool construction and also perhaps an attempt legally to separate the pool business, a riskier one as a business entity, from the other types of construction in which the contractor is engaged.

Pools available in 1960 in Albuquerque were basically of four types of construction. Steel reinforced concrete was available and was the most expensive type. A variation of this was a concrete pool bottom with block sides; the voids in the blocks were filled with concrete and the whole was reinforced with steel bars. A third type was "gunite" in which the concrete and cement are sprayed under pressure on steel mesh. A fourth is a vinyl-liner type. The pool requires the usual excavation, but the sides are made of block or concrete with either a thin concrete or a sand bottom within all of which is suspended a vinyl plastic liner. In 1960 in Albuquerque a firm known as Esther Williams Pool Company was constructing this type of pool with a sand rather than a concrete bottom. These pools have the unique capability of allowing the water to leak out very rapidly if a hole is developed in the liner. If the pool is constructed with a cement bottom, however, the leaks are apt to be less catastrophic. Other types of home pools are the steel tank and molded plastic. But neither of these were or are prominent in the Albuquerque market.

The Vincents secured bids on three types of pools. They desired as large a pool as they could get in the space in their yard and one to fit in their budget. As Chauncey puts it, "We did not want a pool in which people bump heads every time someone dives in." Their yard, being 90 × 150 feet, did not place a severe limitation on the size. Thus, they secured three bids on a 20-foot × 40-foot pool with a maximum depth of about 10 feet. A concrete-type pool would have cost $5900, a gunite pool $5500, a vinyl-liner-type pool $4290. The firm making this last bid was the only one of the three specializing in vinyl-liner pools. Unlike the Esther Williams pool, on which the Vincents did not get a bid, this one did have a concrete bottom so that the pool could, if the desire arose, be converted fairly easily to a nonliner type.

They chose the vinyl-liner pool, but for reasons other than just the fact that it was the lowest bid. As mentioned earlier, Mr. Vincent is a chemist with the AEC. Thus, he claims he was impressed by the salesman's emphasis that with this type pool fewer chemicals were necessary in the water. Algae is less of a problem in vinyl-liner pools than in other types. No alkaline concrete with a rough surface exists to which algae can cling. Less chlorine makes for more comfortable swimming. It was this factor that was apparently even more important than price in their deciding to construct this type.

The firm eventually chosen was at that time the only one in Albuquerque specializing in the vinyl liner with a concrete bottom. The Vincents used the yellow pages of the phone directory to get firms to make bids and did not choose the firm selected on the basis of the recommendation of friends or acquaintances. In fact, they did not then have close friends with a swimming pool from whom to secure information on firms.

The 1960 credit market for pool financing did not differ much from that in 1964. Some financing of pools in Albuquerque in 1960 was done through the contracting firms which then presumably market the paper with a sales finance company. Despite strong rumors in Albuquerque, the Federal Housing Authority does not insure Title One loans on swimming pools. The FHA has taken the position that these loans are for improving the basic livability of a house. Swimming pools are interpreted as a luxury auxiliary. Home savings and loan firms in Albuquerque will lend on pools for the full price up to $3500. Banks now will lend on pools but insist on a one-third down payment. Although financing in 1964 seems a bit easier than in 1960, it is still not as simple as financing an automobile, which often costs as much as a pool and which suffers physical deterioration at a faster rate. This absence of relatively easy financing probably places more of a brake on the expansion of home swimming pools than any other single factor.

One firm stated that four-fifths of the pools it constructed were paid for in cash. This either indicates that pools are still largely a part of the life of the very affluent or that financing is arranged elsewhere than through the contractor.

The Vincents financed $2000 of their pool through a bank loan. For this they put up collateral and secured the loan at a relatively low rate of interest. Currently financing runs up to five years on pools, but the Vincents paid off their loan in two years. At the time they were considering the pool, they also considered a new car. The latter purchase was postponed two years until the pool loan was repaid; then the car was purchased. However, it should be pointed out that this is a one-car family and that the car was a used one.

One other matter should be mentioned in connection with financing. We already stated that one factor that pushed them to a decision in 1960 was a large Federal civil service pay increase. This increase put the Vincents just over the edge of the $15,000-and-over income distribution interval. They were within the top 6.2 percent of United States family income receivers in 1960.

Construction of the pool took place in the summer of 1960. It was done by a contractor under the supervision of the city building department whose inspectors stopped the job on several occasions until the contractor complied with the building code. The major problems seemed to come over the frequency of vertical reinforcing rods in the block voids. The contractor was disturbed over these interruptions, but Mr. Vincent was pleased that the city inspector was on the job and expressed this opinion to representatives of the building department. Despite the careful inspection by the city building department, one deviation from the plan did occur which, as will be seen, made for serious complications that have not been resolved yet. The pool within which the vinyl liner fits was made 8 inches too wide, 9 inches too long, and about 12 inches too deep. The city building department was not impressed by this fact as their primary concern was over conformance of the basic structure to building code strength requirements. At the time the Vincents were convinced by the contractor that this was of no serious consequence because vinyl when warm becomes very pliable and is easily stretched. A liner as large as theirs does have several inches of play, but the amount called for in this instance was extreme to say the least.

The pool was completed and accepted by the end of August, but was not filled until September. This left a very short season of swimming as it is generally too cold for much swimming in Albuquerque after the first of October. No provision was made in the initial construction for heating the water so that the season could be extended.

In the summer and fall of 1960 expectations and anticipations were high. But this was muted shortly by the first difficulties. The contractor went into bankruptcy and while in bankruptcy committed suicide. In the bankruptcy proceedings it turned out that he had not paid all of the bills he incurred in building the Vincent's pool. Under New Mexico law the creditors have a mechanics' lien against the buyer who may already have made full payment under the original contract.[3] The term *mechanics' lien* seems to indicate that it is primarily to protect working men whose wages have not been paid. Its effect is otherwise. It mainly protects suppliers of materials and subcontractors who have not been paid. In this case the Vincents were liable to these subcontractors for approximately $900 that ultimately raised the price of the pool to almost $5200, which is just $300 less than the original bid on a "gunite" pool.

---

[3] Ironically in the May 1960 issue of *Consumer Reports* is a letter in response to the article on swimming pools cited above. The writer was from California. He commented that *Consumers Union* in its article neglected to mention that a prospective buyer of a pool should check to learn whether the contractor is bonded. He then recounted his experience, which, with the possible exception of the amount involved, was identical with that of the Vincents. This letter was indexed in the twelve-month *Cumulative Index* in the June 1960, *Consumer Reports*. Had the Vincents checked the index of this publication under "swimming pools" any time subsequent to the appearance of this issue they most certainly would have come across this cryptic warning.

They did seek legal aid on this problem. But they had no legal recourse except to pay the $900. The contractor was not bonded. No one had explained to them the legal aspects of an unbonded contractor, and they did not know enough about the law to check to see if he was bonded. They feel today that the bank from whom they received a collateral loan failed to explain this quirk of New Mexico law. One recourse did remain to them, however. They could sue the estate of the deceased contractor for recovery of the $900. But since it was bankrupt, the source of their troubles originally, this would be only a ceremonial gesture at best.

This contractual problem was only one of several unforeseen consequences. Sometimes one hears that individuals who install a pool have all kinds of problems with routine maintenance, with intruders, both adult and youthful ones, but these have not been the major consequences that the Vincents have had.

They feel that maintenance is not either financially heavy nor disproportionately time consuming. More time is required in early spring and summer than later in the season. This is because of the blowing sand that is peculiar to Albuquerque at that time of the year. The winds carry not only the sand, but also some trash and leaves. A cover does cut down the amount of cleaning necessary, but this obviously cannot be on all of the time. Thus, early in the season about three cleanings a week are necessary. Two of these take about one hour and a Saturday cleaning takes about two hours. However, in the tranquil days of summer and early fall cleaning is reduced to about one hour a week.

The routing maintenance costs have been fairly low. The Vincents estimate the water costs to be no greater than their water costs prior to the pool. They average about $5 a month. This situation may be unique to the desert Southwest, however. Before the pool was installed, the space was covered with grass. It should be pointed out that in Albuquerque, with an average annual rainfall of slightly more than eight inches, watering of yards goes on all year long. The Vincent's pool is one in which the water is recirculated through a filtration system. The only appreciable loss is that from evaporation, which is probably no greater than the amount of water put on a grassed-in area the size of the pool. In the winter with the pool covered the rate of evaporation is minimal.

Electricity costs have been about $15 for a season. The biggest single item is for chemicals, that cost about $40 per season. It is necessary to use one cup of granular chlorine each day, which is the major source of chemical expense. In sum, the additional cost of operating the pool is between $55 and $60 per season.

The property taxes have been increased as a result of the pool, but since for taxation purposes property is valued at 16 percent of assessed valuation, a pool addition of this type does not increase property taxes very much. Even if the assessed valuation of the property were increased by the full purchase price, the maximum increase in property taxes would be about $50 per year at the present Bernalillo County tax rates.

Costs of routine operation and taxes have not been prohibitive to the Vincents despite the often heard comment that this is one of the unforeseen consequences of a pool. One other lament one hears is that the pool owner is deluged with visitors, both children and adults; however, neither have been a problem to the Vincents. From the beginning the rule on children was that they must be able to swim four lengths of the pool in order to come in without an adult. If a child cannot swim, he must come with one parent. The children of only one family consistently violated this rule, but these were children who, prior to the pool, were accustomed to free and open access to the Vincent yard. The problem was solved simply and easily by having Carol Ellen teach them to swim. One mother did object to the rule, but this was solved when the objecting family built a pool of its own.

Other precautions have been taken. The pool is completely enclosed by a block wall and the house. Entrance to the pool is either through the house or through a storeroom at the rear of the garage, the doors of which can be kept locked. In the event these precautions are not adequate the Vincents do carry a public liability policy on their home, which includes the pool.

Adults have not been a problem. Neither neighbors nor friends have taken advantage of Vincent's hospitality. All seem only to come over for a swim when invited. Chauncey said that, some do not even come when invited. The notion often expressed that a swimming pool brings on more complicated interfamily relations than those that plague a nation has not been true in this case.

But if the usual problem forecast for pool owners has not been experienced by the Vincents, they have had others. Liners do have advantages as far as chemicals are concerned, but they have other disadvantages. They do tear and do develop holes. While this makes patching more difficult than he had hoped, it is not as serious as one might think. The weight of the water keeps the liner snugly against the sides and bottom of the pool at all times. Thus, leaks do not mean a sudden and startling loss of water. Water does leak out because neither the sides nor bottom are waterproof. But the leakage is so slow that one can at times accumulate several leaks before draining the pool to do the patching.

More serious, however, on this score was the original error of the builder in making the pool slightly oversize for the liner. Since the liner is stretched beyond capacity, serious leaks have developed at the corners. In the corners the liner does not adhere tightly to the sides near the top of the pool. But it is just here that it is under greatest tension from stretching. The liner tore in the corners at the deep end of the pool, and since it does not adhere closely to the sides, water poured in between the liner and the block sides of the pool structure. In this case the breaks were serious ones.

The tears in the southwest corner of the pool have been so severe that it was necessary two years ago to have a plastic repair firm vulcanize the corner; unfortunately, the material they used had practically no elasticity. Tears have continued to develop in the corner. At one time in 1963 Chauncey drained the pool and removed the liner in order to build up the corners with concrete. He had the idea that if he rounded the corners in this fashion he could fill the void between the liner and the sides at the corners. He felt this would reduce tension on the liner and also eliminate the hazard of having water get between the liner and the pool wall when leaks developed. This solution has been only partially successful.

At this same time he repaired the bottom, which had developed a lacework of fine cracks and repaired many small holes in the bottom of the liner. Replacing the liner, however, was not easy. It is supposed to be a very simple operation. But because of the necessity of stretching this to fit in each corner, it is a job requiring the help of at least one other person and preferably two.

At this point the liner in the pool is such a problem from having torn and having been patched that the Vincents have considered replacing it; this is, however, not a minor expense. A liner 20 feet × 40 feet costs about $500. In the spring and summer 1964 Montgomery Ward catalogue liners this size are listed at $449 plus shipping charges for one weighing 225 pounds.

An alternative to replacement of the liner is to have the pool converted to a gunite one. This would also be quite expensive. One pool construction firm will convert for three quarters of the original cost of the pool. This price is, however, for guniting the sand-bottom type. For the Vincent's pool it would be somewhat less since it already has a concrete bottom; but Chauncey has recently learned that the pool can be converted by applying a finish of very hard waterproof plaster. This could be done for about $300. The decision has not been made and even though the latter would be cheaper than a new liner, Chauncey is still attracted by the absence of algae in a liner-type pool. So far nothing has been done except discuss at intervals with Ellen the pros and cons of the alternatives available.

In Albuquerque swimming outdoors is largely confined to the period May 15 to September 15 although Chauncey has been in the pool every year as late as the first week of October. In view of the amount of sunshine year round in Albuquerque, one might be surprised of the shortness of the season. But Albuquerque is too high to approximate the mild winters characteristic of Phoenix. Even with a relatively warm sun on winter days the temperature is apt to be near or below freezing and may get close to zero at night.

Although the Vincents did know this, they thought they might lengthen the swimming season by installing an inexpensive heating system that made use of the sun. Chauncey installed a long series of copper coils on the roof of the house through which to run the water from the filtration mechanism before re-entering the pool. He thought the sun would warm the water passing through the coil. But this has not been too effective because of the relatively low heat of the coil and the proportionately small volume of heated water entering the pool.

Another disappointment was the inability to make much use of the pool at night in the summers. Albuquerque is not only high, it is desert as well. The altitude is 5000 feet and diurnal range of temperature is about 30 degrees in the summer. Even though the temperature may reach 100 degrees during a July day, it will probably fall to 70 and 65 at night. During the summer at noon a swimmer may get chilled when he gets out of the water because of the very rapid rate of evaporation in the dry air. At night with the temperature drop and the rapid rate of evaporation, swimming is uncomfortable. Dreams of warm summer evenings around a pool vanished in the reality of the desert climate. Thus, the pool has not been used as much as the Vincents first anticipated. Neither the swimming season nor the swimming day is as long as they thought each might be.

Such a large investment as a swimming pool could be expected to have some effect on the pattern of family activity. Yet in the case of the Vincents this seems to have been at a minimum and what change took place over the subsequent four years may be ascribed more to age changes and concomitant interest changes in the children than to the pool. The family is one who enjoys summer camping, for instance. This they have continued to do despite the pool. Nor have they felt uneasy about leaving home for short camping trips. The first full summer they had the pool they did stick close to home, taking only a one-week camping trip. And on this occasion they did have another family stay in their home in order to keep an eye on the pool. But they now have a pool cover that can be locked in place and they feel no need for daily vigilance.

After four years would the Vincents do it again? They feel that they would and do not regret the investment. When facing some new problem or an old one with the liner Chauncey is apt to state, "This was the worst mistake I made in my whole life." But this is probably an expression of momentary exasperation, for, when asked in a calmer moment what he would do if free to choose again, he states that he feels it was a wise expenditure. He is also convinced that his original choice of a liner-type pool was a correct one despite his difficulties. These he attributes to the original size error made by the contractor.

Often pools are viewed as largely status symbols. It is doubtful that status considerations had much to do with this pool. The owners, despite their place in the top 6.2 percent of the income receivers in 1960 lead a rather modest life. Their home is in a neighborhood in which the assessed valuations are in the $12,000 to $15,000 category. They are a one car family and consistently buy a used car. While they live well enough, they are not social entertainers. The pool is largely a center of family recreation. Undoubtedly status implications are involved in all choices by all peoples, but they are sometimes primary motives and sometimes of far less significance. Observing the general standard of living maintained by this family as well as the manner in which the pool is used, status is of minor significance in this case.

8 / Introduction to WHY I BOUGHT A VOLKSWAGEN

This case concerns the circumstances under which James M. Todd determined to buy a Volkswagen in 1957, the year in which the Volkswagen boom seriously began. The Todds "needed" a second car; a close friend had a VW; the national trend toward such cars was up, up, up toward 8 percent of the market.

At the time that Colonel Todd bought his Volkswagen, such behavior was still moderately innovative. There were few VW's on the road, and the national advertising campaign had not begun. Of course, he was not in the first innovational wave, and the numerous kinds of experience and evidence that he collected before deciding to purchase the car suggests that he is not the sort of person who would be likely to be first in trying out something new. His friend, with a history that included strafing missions with a bomber, seems more the type to be found in the first wave of adopters.

From the standpoint of the marketer there is quite probably no adoption group as important as that represented by Todd. Willing to make a change, even a fairly major one, he is no seeker of the novel. The change must be evaluated and considered both intellectually and emotionally.

He attempts here to give a careful account of the influences and experiences that helped him move toward the purchase of the Volkswagen. Many of these are undoubtedly quite different from the individual experiences of others in the large second wave of adoption, but they must be in some sense comparable.

In effect, the case is one concerning the ways in which information influences attitude change. Todd suggests that personal friends played a major role in his change and the editorial content in the mass media was an important adjunct. One might ask how much of this effect could have been accomplished by any other means.

WHY I BOUGHT
A VOLKSWAGEN

James M. Todd, *Chairman, Department of Management*
Memphis State University

In 1957 I bought a Volkswagen for use as a second car for myself and my family. It was not the first time we had owned a second car; we knew of the additional expense involved and of the advantages of having two cars. In other words, the decision was not influenced by any unknowns connected with the decision of an individual to make the step from one to two cars.

For the purpose of background, 1957 was before the time that compact cars were introduced by the major American automobile manufacturers. At the time, demand for the Volkswagen in the United States was high, and I paid a premium price for an "almost new" car rather than taking my place on a waiting list. There was a plentiful supply of American cars available and no waiting would have been necessary to buy a new or used domestic car.

American automobile manufacturers and marketing analysts had made studies to determine what type of people were buying the imported cars. The findings of these studies were well publicized and one conclusion appeared to be that this was a fad that wouldn't last. References were made to the failure of earlier small cars to attract buyers in any numbers. At the same time, however, our car manufacturers were making plans to introduce compacts that would compete with the foreign cars. Volkswagen was, and I believe still is, the leading import, followed by Renault.

This paper is an attempt to determine the influences that prompted me to buy a Volkswagen, a German-made car, for use as a second car here in the United States.

In order to set the stage for this evaluation it seems necessary to give some idea of my personal history and status at and shortly before the time of purchase.

In 1957 I was thirty-seven years old and came from a middle-class family in a small town in Alabama. I was married and the father of an eleven-year-old son. I was a member of the United States Air Force and had served a total of seventeen years. In addition to normal tours of duty in the United States I had been stationed in England, Alaska, and Korea. Financially my family would, I believe, be considered middle class. We owed no major debts and like many families in our category, we were setting aside as much as possible in savings of one sort or another.

Late in the summer of 1957 I had disposed of my previous second car and had no definite conscious plans for buying another one. As a result, I was riding back and forth to work with a person who lived in my neighborhood. I was doing this only at my wife's insistence and frankly considered the man with whom I was riding as being a little peculiar. This was not my first experience in sharing the ride, I had done it before and didn't like it. Looking back, I believe the reason was because I didn't care to listen to or participate in the conversation and small talk inherent in a car pool, especially in the mornings. Unconsciously there was a desire to use this early morning time in organizing or at least thinking about what would be happening during the day. Not having to share a ride gave me a sense of getting free and resisting coercion and restriction. This establishes one need that influenced me and that together with other factors led to the purchase of another second car.

During the last half of 1957 I do not remember any formal advertising in the mass media by Volkswagen. The majority of the publicity seemed to spring from various articles by columnists in the newspapers attempting to explain who in America was buying the imports. They also attempted to explain why these cars were being bought and what American manufacturers should do.

One article particularly stands out in my memory. In reporting the results of a marketing survey this article showed that the higher income and social status groups were buying the imports at that time. Since this article stands out in my memory I think it would be safe to say that imports in general were becoming, probably unconsciously, somewhat of a status symbol to me.

The mass media stated that Volkswagen was the import being bought in the largest numbers and indicated: (1) It was probably the best of the imports, and (2) there were waiting lists to get one. Articles of this sort were, I believe, influencing me, unconsciously, to buy a Volkswagen. The need was still forming—no definite decision to buy another second car had been made.

Two things happened that finally and definitely influenced me toward the purchase of a Volkswagen.

The first event was taking a demonstration ride in a Volkswagen. I was pleased with the performance, but that was not the whole story. The owner of the local Volkswagen agency was also a member of the Air Force. He was my peer and his recommendation carried more weight than would that of some other person. I didn't think of him as an automobile salesman but as someone from my own social subculture, someone with similar problems and aspirations.

The second event was finding an old friend who was stationed at the same base. He owned a Volkswagen. He was well pleased with it. Naturally, we talked about the car. I heard stories of good handling, low gas consumption, and general high quality. I also heard of a trip from Maine to Mississippi with his wife and boys. I drove his car on several occasions.

As a result of this sequence of events I was satisfied that the Volkswagen was a good car and that it was different and "fun" to drive.

In view of the influence this friend was exerting, several questions need to be asked and answered. How did this particular friend fit into my environment? Why was he my friend? What were my personal opinions of him and of his family? Why was I influenced by him?

Physically he is a big man who has had to watch his weight continually to pass physical examinations. Our acquaintance began at the start of our Air Force careers although we were not close friends at that time. Our paths crossed many times before the present episode. His original home was also in the south. He is extremely independent and outspoken. His blunt mannerisms have not furthered his career.

One of the histories of the Pacific area during World War II contains a typical example of his independence. It mentions him as one of the few pilots who ever flew a four engine bomber down to tree-top level to strafe an enemy-truck convoy.

Our friendship during the latter part of 1957 became much closer, because both of us were newly arrived at the base and neither of us had any other old friends located there.

Shortly after this reunion, I determined to buy a VW. I could picture myself at the wheel and almost sense my new independence from the car pool. But buying a Volkswagen was delayed by circumstances. I could not quite make the decision to spend the money when the satisfaction of having the car remained fairly distant. The local agency predicted at least a seven-month delay between order and delivery.

My indecision lasted until the latter part of December when we were visiting my brother and his family in another city. During the last three days of this visit I went to the local Volkswagen agency to see if any better delivery could be arranged only to find that it could not. Then an alternative was offered when the dealer showed me a clean, used Volkswagen of the current year's model. In 1957 a good used car like this was seldom seen. I drove the car, examined it closely, and decided it was in excellent condition.

A means of early satisfaction of my need was now available and I was forced to make the decision on spending the money. Very little time remained for any further procrastination on this decision since I would be leaving town shortly. The final conscious decision had to be made. We held a family consultation and made the decision to buy. After some partially successful bargaining, I became the owner of a 1957 Volkswagen.

This final action occurred after approximately four months of mental and physical involvement. The actual decision to buy was not made until a means of immediate satisfaction of the need became available. I feel that I would have been willing to postpone the decision much longer if a car had not been for immediate sale. I have owned the car since then completely satisfied with my decision.

9 / Introduction to THE PEACH-FACED PARROT

Not many people own peach-faced parrots, small hooked-beaked birds a bit larger than parakeets. One of them explains, largely in his own words, why he not only bought this bird but a number of others, as well as a variety of pets, including a horse. He really wanted a larger parrot.

Probably no single aspect of consumer behavior is so difficult to understand as the consumer himself. His adjustment to the world and the dynamics of his behavior are seldom simple. The purchases he makes and the way he uses these purchases may be important elements in an analysis of his personality or his future behavior. The archeologist has little to go on beyond the artifacts of a civilization in his inferences about human life in other periods. Yet current practice in the behavioral sciences is generally to disregard the material goods with which the individual surrounds himself. The relevance of consumer goods can possibly be seen a bit more clearly in the unusual rather than the usual purchase.

In the current case, it is easy to see the way in which animals and birds fill some ongoing need of Paul's. In fact, there is considerable evidence that he uses such purchases creatively, not to satisfy a single desire of some sort but to handle some complex of wants, interests, and dissatisfactions. There are obviously status aspects in his approach to birds. But there is little evidence that this is dominant. He seems to experience some sort of sheer, childish delight in watching young parakeets climbing around in a make-believe castle at the five-and-ten that makes him buy one despite the fact that there is nothing special about a parakeet.

Talking about the purchase of a peach-faced parrot, which he enjoys sitting and watching at breakfast time, Paul brings up the purchase of horses, dogs, a variety of finches, and other birds. Without going into a speculative analysis of what pets mean to Paul or people in general, it seems useful to point out that they apparently serve some sustaining function not unlike the coin collection of the numismatist or the pigments and canvas of the Sunday painter. They are at least something into which excess energies can be rewardingly poured.

It seems likely that a well-developed theory of consumer behavior would be useful not only to marketers but to the social sciences as well in the general effort to understand all human behavior. Further, the framework within which consumer behavior lies may make it inherently more available to some sorts of research and analysis than any other form of behavior.

One interesting way in which to view a case like this, in which the personality of the consumer is the matter of focus, is to ask oneself questions about other aspects of his behavior. What kind of sales manager does Paul make? Is he the kind of person who would buy a Buick? How would you go about trying to sell him a life insurance policy? What aspects of his personality should be defined in order to determine his reaction to an advertising campaign? Questions of this sort will suggest the directions that personality theory most applicable to consumer behavior might take.

THE PEACH-FACED PARROT

W. T. Tucker, *Department of Marketing, University of Texas*

Paul is the manager of a sales office of a national organization that produces industrial goods. He has worked for the company about eighteen years in the cities of New York and Philadelphia, starting as a salesman. Like most successful salesmen, he is enormously concerned with service his company gives its customers and works strenuously to see that delivery schedules are kept, that the product lives up to specifications, and that favorable credit arrangements and pricing be maintained. In many ways he is as much the customer's representative to his own company as he is the company's district sales manager; and, like most sales managers, he spends a large portion of his time taking care of accounts that are important to the office.

He lives well, as successful sales executives do. His home is a handsome, older home with more bedrooms and baths than the family can use. Like most of the homes in the better residential areas of the Philadelphia suburbs, it is on a large, tree covered lot. He has a wife and three teenage sons, all of whom are fitted out with fanciful nicknames supplied by Paul. The nicknames vary a bit from year to year so that they won't become too routine; the result is that everyone in the house has a collection of four or five nicknames, all used interchangeably.

Paul is an excellent raconteur and can slip easily into several modes of speech or dialects. His favorite is a slightly personalized Runyanese with its characteristic present tense referring often to either the past or future. He is completely gregarious and enjoys discussing almost any matter with almost anyone. Of course, he loves to strike up new acquaintances, especially with people to whom there has been no introduction. Such new-found friends are likely to be endowed with a nickname during the first hour or so. He has considerable charm and argues gaily, taking any contentious view that is available, since agreement can be quite dull.

His mannerisms are extremely masculine. And he has much of the athletic ability about which he may boast delightedly in the classic masculine fashion. He played a fairly good brand of high school football at 150 pounds, is a fine bowler (and part-owner of bowling lanes), and can outdrive most golfers by something more than a few yards. He reads considerably more than one might expect if one were trying to see him as the average sales executive.

This is the story of his purchase of a peach-faced parrot. A considerable portion of it will be in his own words, taken from a tape recording.

I went in this place, which I'd been in before. Their stock is fairly extensive so that there is a good number of people in there, both buying and not buying. I went in and no one paid particular attention to me, probably because there were enough things there that I was looking around myself. Perhaps I didn't look like I was specifically interested in purchasing something.

So, shortly I went over to one of these guys and asked him if he could help me, and he averred he could. I said, "I saw your ad on these peach-faced parrots, and I want to buy one." So he says, "Well, they're fun to hear." And I say, "I know they are, I see them and I watch them." So we walk up to the front together and look over these various ones flying around. And he says, "Do you have any preference?" And I say, "Yes, I like that one." It looks like a young bird; actually, I think they are all young birds.

This one appealed to me. He caught it and brought it back, and then he said, "Have you ever had a peach-faced parrot?" I said, "No." So then he said, "You'll need a cage." I said, "I have a cage." He said, "Do you know what to feed it?" I said, "Roughly, yes." He said, "You'll need food." I said, "Yes." So he sold me a mixture for parrots with kinds of seeds and pepperies in it, which, incidentally, they don't eat. He sold me a bag of sunflower seeds, which they like. Peanuts, they throw them all out.

He said, "You're going to have a bath for the bird." I said, "I have that," which I didn't. But I know you can put in a little thing of water every now and then which will do just as well. He said, "You ought to have this kind of feeder." I said, "I have that," which again I didn't. But it was the old sales jump. But he did sell me several additional articles, including a little book, which I wanted anyway. It was *Parrots and Parrotlike Birds.* I bought it because it has various disease symptoms and things like that. So I purchased this, too. Besides the thirty bucks I paid for the bird, I would say I spent another five bucks on various accessories, even though I had the cage. I bought this bird at noon. So I went back to the office and worked the afternoon. Although I had paid and had everything set up prior to the time, I didn't actually pick the bird up, nor did he take the bird out of the display until I went back.

The advertisement for peach-faced parrots had been in the sports section of the morning paper, a section that Paul reads regularly. Beyond that he had built up something of a habit of looking at the advertisements of the pet store from which he bought the bird, because they often advertised exotic pets.

I have frequently been interested in their ads. For instance, they run a special, say, on squirrel monkeys. $14.95 for a little squirrel monkey, see. And, again, I would have gone in and bought the thing, but I know my situation here and everything. Oh, hell, that'd be the last thing in the world I had better do, so I have resisted.

But besides reading the advertisements, Paul had become familiar with the pet store, stopping to look in the windows and even going inside.

Well, you can't walk up Market Street and not see a group of people around the window. As a pet shop, it is very commercially-minded. One window, the first time I went in, had a bird display, not in cages, but the whole window set up on an aviary basis. And in the other window they had—what do you call those things? They're not gila monsters, but they're . . . iguanas.

A fair number of the people go inside, which I did. In other words I said, if they have this outside, what have they got inside? I go in and they do, they have a very, very complete assortment as far as a pet shop goes. Usually you walk in and they have mainly supplies. Maybe some fish, or they may have some canaries or some parakeets. But this place is very *extensively* stocked.

Of course, none of this really explains why Paul went in to buy the peach-faced parrot when he saw the advertisement. Several other factors were operating. First, he had an empty cage, which will take some explanation of itself. Second, he has an enormous interest in and affection for animals that can be traced back to fairly early childhood. Third, the bird was an interesting compromise. It was larger than a parakeet and rarer without being much larger, more expensive, or more trouble. As Paul said:

> What I actually wanted was a full-sized parrot. A yellow-head or something like that. But I've got a relationship with my wife to maintain, and this is a very satisfactory compromise. It doesn't take up the space, it's more docile generally speaking than a true parrot, and it's a pretty little bird, one which with proper handling can do much the same things as a parrot.

Paul first owned a bird when he was about ten years old in 1931, but he remembers earlier associations quite clearly. The mother of a childhood friend bred canaries. One side of their living room was covered with linoleum and the entire wall was covered with cages of canaries. He was interested. But it was not until later, after his family had moved from Wisconsin to the New York suburbs that he had ever seen a parakeet as a pet. And the first ones he saw were two cobalt birds he received as a gift. An aunt who knew that he was interested in pets took him to visit the place of a parakeet breeder who was raising the birds in a former greenhouse. She bought him the pair of birds and a large cage that included a nesting box. The birds bred and Paul helped raise the young parakeets. Occasionally he would visit the woman from whom the birds had been purchased, especially in warm weather when the parakeets were in outdoor flyways. They were of all the usual colors—greens, yellows, blues, and some so pale that they were almost white.

Paul cannot remember anyone in the town in which he was living who had a bird of any kind. The town was made up almost entirely or families headed by a father and husband who commuted to New York and generally worked as a business executive. It may well be that such people, at that particular time, did not keep birds of any sort. But the number of dogs was astronomical. There may well have been as many dogs as families in the town. Irish setters were much the rage. Of course, Paul had a dog. But his parakeets were the curiosity of the neighborhood. People, especially children, friends of Paul's or of his older brother and sister, would drop in particularly to see the birds, which were often allowed to fly free in the house.

During this period an uncle from Los Angeles visited the family and took considerable interest in Paul and his parakeets. When he returned to the West Coast, he purchased three pairs of zebra finches and shipped them back to his nephew. It is not difficult to imagine the reaction of Paul's parents, especially his father, who maintained a fairly successful pretense of gruffness; but they were modern parents in what was probably the first generation to practice permissiveness on a widespread scale. Another large cage and more nesting boxes were purchased.

The dog and the birds were not all. Paul also had an aquarium and tropical fish. It is worth pointing out that his attitude is not really the same toward the various sorts of pets he had. Fish were to him pretty things to look at "the way a woman may look at a bouquet of flowers." And as for the birds:

> They're an attraction, but they're not pets. I think anybody who calls a bird a pet is misnaming him. There's no affection connected to it, and I think the word "pet" connotes affection. Now I know women who have birds and have affection for those birds, and they think the birds return it. That is a lot of nonsense. Birds don't do this. They may appear to because they are hungry or something else. If you have a single bird, that is a different situation, too. Maybe the bird gets lonely. But there is no affection such as a dog has.

But in another way there are certain strong, central points-of-view that he holds toward all animals and his relationship to them.

> There again, to me it's part of the—I don't say the challenge. That's probably not the right word. But, if you have living things, you like to involve yourself with the entire cycle—or at least I do. And this carries over even to dogs. I've got this little poodle, and I've mentioned on many occasions that I would like to have another one and actually raise the little things.

> Not for profit. You would sell them merely because you can't become overburdened with them. That wouldn't be my primary purpose. My primary purpose, I don't want to sound maudlin. But these little things were put here to perform the same function that we are, which is to reproduce themselves. I kind of like to help it along. And, again, it's nothing I can really explain. If anybody said to me, "What the hell do you want six dogs for instead of two or ten birds instead of two?" it's nothing that you can give a very valid answer to. And yet, within me, that's why I'd like to do it.

When Paul was about fifteen or sixteen, the maid left a window open, the parakeets got outside, and a cold snap killed them. He can't remember what happened to the finches, but they, too, disappeared during his first year or so of high school. There were no special pets for a number of years, until, in fact, he was in the army during World War II and was located on the West Coast, with his wife trying her best to follow the various moves and counter-moves that military orders dictated.

> I was spending most of my time at the base. My wife was living alone. There was a place out in the San Fernando Valley that had large, wild

animals among other things. It was one of those roadside operations, and they had a puma, racoons, and some foxes. But, they also had a lot of pet-type animals. So I bought another parakeet, a pair of parakeets again. Brought them home. I thought with me away, this would be something for her to do—my thinking, not hers. And, of course, she says, "What the hell, I'm tied down." But she enjoyed them, too. So she has a pair of parakeets. Then she was moving around, and I took them with me in the army. I was sent to Los Angeles to work in the operations room for three months, lived in an apartment with two other officers and had these birds with me.

And then I went back in the field. Of course, I couldn't take the things with me. I gave them to the guy who was going to take my place down town and move into the apartment. That was the end of that one.

Shortly before he was shipped out of the States, Paul ran into an officer who owned a horse, an Irish jumper. Since the other officer was leaving and was willing to sell the horse at a bargain, Paul bought it. It was stabled some distance from camp, but Paul occasionally worked it out. His wife, fond of horses, and a good rider, was somewhat upset by the impracticality of the arrangement. When Paul shipped out to Hawaii, she sold the horse in order to save the stable and feed bills.

During the remainder of the war, Paul remained petless, although he saw a number of interesting varieties of birds on the islands. And after the war, birds did not soon recur. In 1946 he purchased a fawn great dane, which he walked around the new suburban housing development in Connecticut where they had moved. He trained the dog with patience, but before the task was completed, he was forced to spend several months largely away from home in a training program. Since his wife was in the last months of pregnancy, the rambunctious young dane was literally dangerous. Her affection and enthusiasm sent neighboring children, and even adults sprawling. After considerable thought and discussion, Paul sold the dog.

During this period in which his career was beginning, Paul often talked about ranching as a way of life. He and his wife would have serious discussions about the practicalities and impracticalities of making a living in some sort of livestock venture. His wife was certain that no one as gregarious as Paul could settle for the relative loneliness of ranch life. It is not difficult to imagine this conversation, and is likely that most businessmen have at one time or another talked in terms of an occupation different from their own such as running a ski lodge. One often remarked that he thought you could make a living with a sailboat hauling cargo in the West Indies.

A somewhat more concrete possibility for Paul was the breeding of chinchillas. In 1947, chinchilla breeding became quite a fad. Paul wanted to get into the business using a neighbor's garage to start. His hesitancy, and absolute refusal to handle the venture alone, was based on the presumption that the animals would have to be killed and skinned. While willing to take care of the live animals, he drew the line at slaughter. He said that he understood the inconsistencies involved in being willing to have a partner handle that end of the business but being unwilling to do it himself. He was firm. "No one likes roast beef any more than I do," he said. "But, if I had to kill the steers, there wouldn't be any steaks in the A & P. It's as simple as that."

With the Korean War, Paul was put back on active duty and sent to Germany. Household affairs were confused and difficult for a few years with moves, new children, and changing job assignments. Then Paul purchased a grey, toy poodle as a surprise for his wife.

> She's got this poodle that I bought her and often, most often, I find her being affectionate to the dog and so on. But the first sign of trouble and she backs off and never wanted the dog in the first place. I foisted it on her, see? But pets are like children; you take the disadvantages along with the advantages, and the advantages outweigh the disadvantages. But if you're not fond of them, you don't look at it in this light. All you can see is the troublesome side of it.

The poodle is a well-trained dog. Paul has spent hours teaching it tricks and playing with it. His sons have both continued the process and disrupted it somewhat. But the dog is now old.

About five or six years ago, the first of the new birds appeared in a completely fortuitous way.

> Mrs. C had two of these things, both of which she kind of inherited. Two parakeets in separate cages, one a yellow bird and one a yellowish-green. Her husband died, and they sold the home. (Mrs. C moved in for a short time with her son, a neighbor of Paul's, before going south to live.) So there they were. Two birds don't mean a lot. I said I'd be delighted to have those things, so she gave me both of them. This is where I got the two cages, the one that has the peach-face in it and the one that Eddie is in. (Eddie is a yellowish-green parakeet.)

> We went away for the summer and the D's kept them for us. One was Budge's and the other was Mustiferly's (two of the boys by present nomenclature.) We went over to get them, and came across the street with them. Budge stumbled and fell down, the cage came apart, and one flew away. So then I had an extra cage, and this is when I got into the peach-face business.

After a short period of time the peach-faced parrot got out of the cage and flew into a window killing himself. He was replaced by a second peach-faced parrot. And Paul visited the home of one of his salesmen.

> Out on the porch he had a big black cage. It wasn't hanging, it was on a little stand, you know. And it was empty. I said, "What have you got there?" And he said, "Oh hell, we got a canary. And we came out one morning and the bugger has his feet in the air. Now I've got a cage." I said, "I'll buy it from you." He said, "I'll give it to you." I said, "Well, that's no kind of a deal. I'll give you a dollar."
>
> So I bought the cage from him. I got another cage with nothing in it. Of course, I didn't buy the cage to have nothing in it anyway. You don't very often do that. So I went over to this pet place and I looked around. They had only ordinary birds in there, nothing unusual.
>
> On a real off chance, my neighbor had seen my bird and said, "Dotty would just love a bird." And I said, "I'll buy you one." And this time I'd read that Woolworth was selling parakeets for $1.98. So I went down there, and they had all these baby parakeets, tails weren't even fully developed. And they weren't in cages at all. They were in a kind of castle arrangement, running around, you know, and their wings were clipped.
>
> I didn't notice this at the time, but I wondered why these sons-of-guns are tearing around this thing of ladders and ramps, but not flying. So they intrigued me. They were so young I knew they were tameable. So I bought two of them. One for her, and one for me—which wasn't the original plan. I was going to get her a parakeet, which I told her I would do. And when I saw the damn things I bought two of them. And I got another cage free from another friend. Now I'm up to my neck in parakeets.
>
> While I was there, I saw this pintail (whydah). I said, "Where did you get a little bird with a tail like that?" The saleswoman says, "That's a bird of paradise." I said, "Oh, is it now?" And I said, "What's that other?" She says, "That's the female." So I said, "How much is he?" She says, "$9.98." "And how much is the pair," I asked. She says, "9.98." Since the pair was the same price as the male alone, I naturally said I'd take the two. These pintail finches were in a cage—1 male and about 6 females. She gave me a male and a female, and I know enough about birds to know you don't get a mated pair that way. Many, many birds are monogamous. A robin is, for instance. Very definitely, absolutely. Many birds are, and I'm inclined to believe finches are. You cannot just put any two parakeets in a cage and have a mated pair. You can put fifty parakeets in a cage and they'll pick their own mates. And then you've got something. But any two won't just mate offhand like that.

It is always difficult to talk about motives and intentions that may be involved in a purchase. Paul explains the purchase of the peach-faced parrot in several ways, both in terms of his specific plans for the bird and in terms of analogies.

Actually, what I expected to do and what I hoped to do was to finger-tame this bird much in the same way you would a parakeet. To me they have more appeal than a parakeet. I don't know what the intelligence ratio is, but you get the impression from the similarities between this bird and a full-sized parrot that it would have many of the same characteristics. And I think they would show, if you spent the time with it. In fact, I know it would.

As a matter of fact, one of the deals in this ad is the guarantee to talk. If it doesn't talk in six months, bring it back and we'll replace it. Well, I've had this bird considerably longer than six months. It doesn't say a damn word, and I wouldn't think of replacing it.

They know that when the ad is placed; it's part of the psychology. You get attached to it and wouldn't think of replacing it.

I have this secretary in my office who has a parakeet. The thing says full sentences. It says, "Merry Christmas." It will say, "What the hell!" And it says other things. A parakeet, not a parrot. I've never heard it, but she says it's perfectly audible. Now, I've known parrots that say phrases and things and, conversely, I know parrots that don't say a word. I think the whole thing is training. You can take two mutts out of the same litter. You can train one of them to walk on its forefeet and do tricks like that. The other one, if it isn't properly handled, will mess on your living-room floor.

(Concerning the peach-faced parrot) I haven't had the time to devote to him that I would like to have had in the training of any animal. It has got to be a planned, consistent thing. I haven't been able to do it, but he gives me a lot of pleasure. I can sit there at breakfast, mostly on the weekends when I have a lot of time for breakfast, and he is a funny thing, an amusing thing, and a pretty thing.

Out of, I don't know, in this township we probably have 14,000 people. I don't know all of them by any manner of means, but I suppose the fact that I have a peach-faced parrot places me among a very select few. On the other hand, there are a lot of others who have horses, and I don't have a horse. This isn't practical for me.

I'll probably have horses again. But living things just appeal to certain people. Most, I would say. As a matter of fact, I'll go even further there. I would say that most people of character have a fondness for living things. They may be plants. H. R. across the street has a rather extensive green-house arrangement where she keeps plants. Unusual plants. And I think this applies to any person. In other words, if you like gardening, you are even happier if you've got plants that other people don't have and better ones. She has orchids and things like that, merely because they are harder to come by; they're harder to raise, and there is more satisfaction in raising them.

If you like animals and birds the way I do, you could have sparrows in a cage. But so could anybody—and this is not just snob appeal or anything like that but an inclination to have something a little different, a little unusual as things go. I mean different and unusual to me. If I can get the plan started, I'd like to have a parrot, and another parrot, and maybe another parrot. Ideally, I'd like to raise parrots, which has never been done in captivity except in one or two exceptional circumstances.

Paul obviously views the peach-faced parrot, the pintail finches, and the remaining parakeet as merely a present situation that will change. In part he feels that he is educating his family, and especially his wife, so that she will not react too strongly to some future parrot or horse. There is little question but that the birds compensate in some way for the more or less irksome aspects of organization life, to which most men are subject. Paul says that he would quit his job immediately, if he could make as good a living raising birds. But he knows that the question, and his answer are both theoretical—and that they will remain so. He explains the answer in the following way:

> By the general standard of things, I have a very good job. But there are aspects of it with which I am in complete disagreement. I mean that through the nature of the position I hold I am doing things which I would not do if I had my own way. Being subject to decisions with which I do not necessarily agree is one thing. Sometimes I don't think they are the best methods by which to operate a business, but some decisions are not mine to make. If I were doing this other thing, I would be doing something I enjoy. And, win, lose, or draw, I would be on my own.
>
> Don't get me wrong, I like my work, and I make some of the decisions. But that is a different thing.

No brief treatment of this sort can explain an individual or a purchase he makes. Paul is enthusiastic about his company and most of its practices. He is enthusiastic about the San Francisco Giants. He likes to Indian wrestle with his sons. He likes to bet on the meaning of words, on matters of fact such as the location of a river or the number of cattle in India, on baseball games, or on a golf match in which he is a participant. He likes to see his wife well-dressed and often insists that she buy new clothes, perhaps in part because she is extremely handsome and dresses with flair. He plays an enthusiastically aggressive brand of bridge. He likes children, and animals and automobiles. Also, he happens to like birds.

10 / Introduction to BOB PALMER'S PREFERENCE IN BEER

Bob Palmer, a former resident of the St. Louis area, drinks Budweiser and Michelob almost exclusively. The case relates his preference to his former life in that area and to his present social situation as a law student.

Pullin's case could be discussed as the evidence that an individual chooses his products as a part of a continuing search for identity. Bob Palmer lives in a changing world in which fathers die and children grow up and move away to pursue their own careers. At twenty-three years of age he is not yet sure who he is. Although living in Oklahoma, he does not want to be mistaken for a "Sooner."

As a child he undoubtedly imitated his uncle in many ways. Perhaps he still walks like him or has other small mannerisms picked up from his example of what a boy is supposed to grow into. In part, his preference for Budweiser is imitative. Such an imitative action can become merely habitual and lose any contemporary meaning. (One may learn to tie his shoes by imitating his mother without the act of tying shoes having any particular symbolic character.) It is no such simple habit that supports Bob's beer preference.

When Bob orders a beer by brand, the very act probably reassures him that he is actually Bob Palmer of Webster Grove, Missouri, a young man on the way to matching the success of his uncle. He must suffer a bit more than his share of anxiety or he would hardly go to such lengths as to describe his brand of beer as the beer of successful businessmen. He knows perfectly well that the brand of beer he drinks will have little to do with his success. But calling for it by name, and drinking it in temporary escape from the rigors of law school has become as symbolic and probably as satisfying as the wearing of a class ring or fraternity pin.

This is one context in which brand loyalty may be high. The analysis seems to raise two questions. First, is there anything inherently unsatisfac-

116

tory in an individual leaning on a brand image that helps him adjust to demanding circumstances? Second, is this the usual form brand loyalty takes or may brand loyalty serve other sorts of use?

BOB PALMER'S PREFERENCE
IN BEER

Jerald L. Pullins

Bob Palmer has lived all of his life in Webster Grove, Missouri, a suburb of St. Louis. He is twenty-three years old and is a first-year student at The University of Oklahoma Law School. Webster Grove is composed of families who have above average or high incomes; as a result, many of Bob's acquaintances are professional people and nearly all are college graduates.

Bob's father was killed in World War II, and due to family problems, he has lived since that time with an uncle, who is a dermatologist. However, Bob has remained very close to his mother. Bob describes his "family" as his mother, sister, aunt, and uncle. He intends to finish law school and possibly continue school for a degree in business.

Bob frequently purchases two brands of beer, Budweiser and Michelob. The products are obviously different in two ways. First, Michelob is always priced slightly higher than Budweiser. In fact, Michelob is one of the highest priced, American-brewed beers sold in the United States. Budweiser is usually priced 5 percent to 25 percent below Michelob. The second obvious difference is in the containers. Michelob is sold in distinctive bottles or on draft and is not sold in cans. Budweiser is sold in both cans and ordinary export bottles. Beyond these two tangible distinctions, the difference between the two beers varies according to the person describing them. Budweiser and Michelob are both brewed in St. Louis by Anheuser-Busch, Inc., and are distributed in the same geographic areas.

Bob usually states a preference for Budweiser, except when he is in a bar or club where Michelob is on tap. Wherever it is possible to order Michelob on tap, Bob prefers it to Budweiser. He seldom deviates from this pattern of behavior.

Immediately after his father was killed, Bob went to live with his uncle, Pete Palmer in Webster Grove. Bob was four years old at the time. Pete is a respected specialist and has enjoyed considerable success in his field. Bob regards his uncle as a success and thinks very highly of him. Pete has had a considerable effect on Bob in developing his beer preferences. Pete has purchased Budweiser for as long as Bob can remember. Bob remembers his uncle as a Budweiser drinker and believes his uncle started him drinking Budweiser in preference to other brands. Bob's tastes in many areas were formed by observing his uncle. He doesn't feel his uncle has poor taste in any area. It is easy to see how Bob's preference and taste for beer were adopted.

Bob grew up in a liberal atmosphere. A beer before dinner or in the evening was a frequent occurrence, and the beer was always Budweiser. Although Bob recalls that he tried many brands during his early beer-drinking days, the product image that he developed through his association with his uncle has served to strengthen a preference for Budweiser. In other words, Bob subconsciously gets more out of Budweiser than the taste.

Living in St. Louis was also conducive to developing a taste for Budweiser and Michelob. Anheuser-Busch, Inc., along with several other large breweries, is located in St. Louis. The brewing industry is one of St. Louis' most respected, well-known industries.

Anheuser-Busch, Inc., is even more well-known and respected in St. Louis because August A. Busch owns the St. Louis Cardinal baseball team. Since Bob is an avid Cardinal fan, Budweiser, Anheuser-Busch, August A. Busch, and the Cardinals are frequently mentioned together with favorable connotations. I get the impression that drinking Budweiser reminds Bob of St. Louis baseball. In fact, if baseball is mentioned while Bob is drinking beer he freely associates the two verbally.

Until he was in college, Bob was not encouraged to drink in various bars throughout St. Louis. Not that he was forbidden to drink, but he was encouraged to drink at home or with adults instead of in bars. Bob was almost 19 before he left home and was free to purchase and drink beer without some restraints or fear of reprisal.

Bob belongs to what I term the "old rich" of St. Louis. In other words the Palmers have had a small fortune in the family for several generations. The old rich of St. Louis are very much aware of social norms that prevail and must be followed. One of the main tenents of the social class to which the Palmer family belongs is "thou shalt not show your money." Families who have had wealth for several generations gain more status from tradition than from buying new, expensive articles to show their wealth. For instance, Bob's uncle lives in a house that has been in the Palmer family for several generations, although he could easily afford a new or better one.

Family social position may help explain Bob's purchase of Budweiser. First, the beer is old and accepted in St. Louis. Second, while being accepted as a "quality" or "premium" beer, Budweiser is not the most expensive beer available. Many imported beers or some American brewed beers, such as Michelob, are higher priced. An accepted, quality beer satisfied Bob's social needs.

In high school Bob had lived with his aunt and uncle. He participated very little in high-school activities and did not participate in high-school athletics. In short, his socialization prior to college was built primarily around his home and a small group of friends he had known all his life. This limited interaction with others of his own age group tended to make Bob shy among strangers and somewhat insecure; however, he wanted desperately to be accepted by his friends in college. Bob pledged a social fraternity upon entering the University of Missouri.

At this point in his life Bob began drinking Michelob beer on draft. There are several reasons why Bob switched from being a constant Budweiser drinker to the use of draft Michelob.

First, the almost total acceptance of Budweiser did not prevail in Columbia as it had in St. Louis. In his new environment Bob was confronted with people who preferred many other brands of beer and who had good reasons for their preference. Second, Bob was now in a social group that looked on a trip to the local beer garden as a normal everyday occurrence. Going down to get a beer in the afternoon or evening was an accepted social act. Third, Budweiser was looked upon as simply another of the "good" beers. Other brands such as Schlitz, Coors, Millers, and Falstaff were lumped in the same general class of most of his peers. Fourth, Michelob and several imported beers were generally regarded as the best or highest quality. Drinking Budweiser did nothing to establish an individual's sophisticated taste within the group.

The change of circumstance forced Bob to re-evaluate his standards and tastes for beer. He soon began drinking Michelob on draft. An important aspect of Bob's change to Michelob is that he will not buy Michelob in bottles. However, Bob will occasionally drink Budweiser on draft and he always buys Budweiser in cans or bottles.

But, if Bob thought so much of Michelob, why didn't he drink it all the time and stop buying Budweiser? Here, Bob's old social norms came into play. Bottled Michelob is about 25 percent more expensive than bottled or canned Budweiser. Buying Michelob in bottles might give the impression of "showing your money" and as a member of the "old rich," Bob's ingrown social reflexes were to be a conservative spender. Therefore, Bob justified his position by buying draft Michelob, which is as he states, "about as expensive as bottled Budweiser."

Currently, he frequently makes statements such as, "I've been drinking Bud since my St. Louis days." He refers to Budweiser as his "St. Louis beer." In fact Bob refers to his favorite St. Louis taverns as "Budweiser Bars."

When Bob left St. Louis for college he fully intended to return there after graduating from law school in order to set up a practice. In view of these plans one can understand why Bob has remained very "St. Louis" conscious during college.

After graduating from the University of Missouri, Bob enrolled in the University of Oklahoma School of Law. Since coming to Oklahoma, Bob's preference for Budweiser and Michelob has apparently grown stronger. Like many newcomers to the university, Bob has not willingly adopted many "Sooner" standards and social norms. In other words, the feelings that Bob has held in the past are growing stronger because of the need to justify his purchase decision in a new society. Bob's strong association with Budweiser and Michelob also cause him to perceive local beers as definitely inferior. He calls them "poor quality, cheap, second-rate beers."

At the university Bob is striving hard for social recognition. He perceives Budweiser and Michelob as the two best selling beers among the students, although they probably are not.

Bob's choice between Budweiser and Michelob seems to be affected by the social group and the environment. The more formal an occasion, the more inclined Bob is to purchase Michelob. Bob defines his mood when he is most inclined to purchase Michelob as "expansive." I have observed that "expansive" moods most often occur when there are several people present, when he wants to make an impression on those present or when he has an unusually large amount of change with him. I feel Bob purchases Michelob when the subconscious desire to indicate his social standing is strong.

The advertising of Budweiser and Michelob seems to reinforce the basic needs that Bob has developed. The latest advertising emphasizes "Beechwood Aging." Bob describes this unusual process as giving Budweiser a very distinctive flavor.

I asked Bob to define several of the terms he frequently mentioned as a basis for his preference in beer. He was hard pressed to define: "premium," "quality," "smooth," or "light."

Bob described his preference for Budweiser and Michelob as "an accumulation of taste." He actually feels he has sampled a wide variety of different beers and has chosen Budweiser and Michelob as the best tasting. I describe his preference as an accumulation of social interactions. *At this time,* the values that Bob has placed on Budweiser and Michelob coincide with his concept of his social position.

11 / Introduction to ANOTHER DRESS

This account of Barbara Fleming's purchase of a dress for a homecoming game and dance seems to emphasize the importance of social class and role in the selection of clothing. The fact that she is seventeen, that she is a Negro, that she comes from a feminine household with definite standards of propriety dictate much of her behavior including her choice of stores and some of her preference in clothing.

It would be a mistake to suggest that too much effort has gone into the examination of consumer behavior from the managerial point of view, but certainly too little has concentrated on the ways in which the marketing process affects the consumer. And that little has too often concerned itself with such relatively minor matters as shopping inconvenience and the irritating quality of certain advertising practices rather than broader issues. Yet it is probable that only bold speculation on these broader issues can suggest the full variety of subject matter that needs careful definition and measurement in a satisfactory theory of consumer behavior.

The combination of mass production and mass marketing is surely one of the strong acculturative forces in a nation that has not fully integrated the diverse peoples who compose it into a single, viable social complex. The market provides for Barbara Fleming both the reward system that justifies and supports middle-class values and the sorts of interaction that define those values in behavioral terms.

In effect, the marketing system has played a part in making Barbara Fleming a subtle and unconscious Lysistrata. She is not available to the untrained or delinquent youths of her race. And who would have her must aspire to what she aspires to and must furnish her with evidence that he can provide it. What he must provide, of course, is not just the financial ability to purchase the dress and the bath oil but a set of social interactions comparable in their comfort and ease with those she experiences in the process of purchasing those items. If much less is offered, she will keep her bath oil in her "own little apartment."

Of course, Barbara is not typical in her family background, school, experience, or shopping history.

121

ANOTHER DRESS

W. T. Tucker, *Department of Marketing, University of Texas*

Barbara Fleming is a junior in high school. Alert, talkative, and outgoing, she seems brighter than the numerous tests taken by students declare her to be. In the tenth grade they placed her generally in the lowest fifth of her age group. She is rated in the lowest tenth in verbal comprehension. The tests are probably a poor measure of her native intelligence, though not as inaccurate as they would be for a Negro from a less well-to-do home.

Barbara lives with two career women who earn respectable salaries: her aunt, who is a registered nurse, and her aunt's friend, a secretary to a local Negro businessman. Barbara's mother died more than ten years ago, and her father placed the child with his older sister. The two women have created the special middle-class world in which Barbara has been raised—first with dreams of becoming a doctor, which have faded to be replaced by the idea of life as a teacher, and second, with the standards of propriety appropriate to the middle class. Barbara is not allowed to borrow or lend clothes. She is quizzed carefully before she is allowed out at night, with either boys or girls of her own age. Prior to a date (she has about three a month), she and the boy she is going out with receive what Barbara refers to as "the lecture." It starts with the announcement that Barbara is a nice girl, that she is due in at a particular time (this varies according to the occasion but tends to be a bit earlier than is usual for girls of her age), and it concludes with the suggestion that another date may be permitted if both teenagers behave well.

Barbara knows that all dates or other outings are merely tentative until this ordeal is finished satisfactorily. Either of her aunts (she calls her aunt's friend "aunt") may decide that she cannot go out with a particular boy or girl or at a particular time when Barbara is standing at the door, ready to leave. As Barbara says, "I am sure about it only when the door closes behind me."

Barbara is discouraged from wearing the kinds of "sloppy" clothes common to teenage girls on weekends or after school. One of her friends is an example of how not to dress in her cutoffs and sweatshirt, although they live close together and are of the same social class. Barbara is sensitive to social-class differences and likes to refer to family size in her neighborhood.

"All the families there have only one child or none." And she refers with frequency to the occupations of the parents. "You know, they are mostly lawyers and doctors and like that."

Of course, she sees herself as unique. "I," she says casually, "am the big mystery!" She does not mean that she fails to understand her own motives or intentions. She means simply that no one, neither "aunts" nor school-teachers nor friends, has yet come close enough for true intimacy. Hers is not an unusual state for a somewhat introspective teenager: the world insists upon dealing with superficial aspects of her behavior rather than with *her*. She is not fully aware of the extent to which her character and her goals have been shaped by that world.

When she was quite young, the doctor for whom her aunt worked used to visit the home. He would throw Barbara in the air and catch her, saying, "What is my little polecat going to grow up to be?" Barbara would answer, "I'm going to be a doctor, and a better one than you." The routine was jovial, filled with masculine humor, but it encouraged an aggressiveness seldom appropriate in a household of women intent on clinging to respectability. The aggressiveness of her "aunts," both spinsters, and its direction must have been clear to her from an early age. But much of it was couched in terms of propriety and service. When Barbara discovered that becoming an M.D. was a literal impossibility, she decided to set her sights on a career as a teacher. The impossibility of her earlier childish commitment did not become obvious at an early date. Barbara knew of women doctors, knew a Negro woman physician of some repute. The early schools she attended did not give her an adequate estimate of her own abilities which must, at times, have seemed large. For the first several years of grammar school she attended a Roman Catholic parochial school after the fashion of the children of middle-class Negro families in a neighborhood which was interested in both the academic and behavioral standards of the school.

On transfer to public school Barbara was somewhat ahead of her class and thought of herself as an extremely capable student. But after six months, new material began to make her relative competence clear, although she didn't really understand what had happened. She still thought of herself as someone who knew it all and who didn't need to work. Her grades failed to show her inadequacies and were, in fact, relatively high. "In junior high school," she says, "I sort of lived off my folk's name." She began to realize that she was receiving high grades no matter what sort of work she did. In one class her work was automatically given an A, because the teacher thought highly of Barbara's aunt.

During the four years from fifth through eighth grades she was in predominantly Negro schools, learning little and coming to understand with increasing clarity that she was not being prepared for the sort of life she had been taught to anticipate. Her "aunts" were concerned with the situation and transferred her to a well-run high school that was predominantly white. As Barbara says, "I found that I couldn't do exactly what I thought I could. And, from then on I said I wanted to be a teacher where I could prepare the kids—not give them grades because they are cute or because of their mother or daddy, but because of what they do."

Barbara's is no vigorous sense of mission. But she needs to feel personally valuable in the terms of her own household where it is impossible to maintain unrealistic dreams of a future as a physician. She hopes to teach fourth or fifth grade, in part because it was at this stage that her own educational process was critically altered, in part because she recognizes that she probably cannot acquire the education necessary to teach at higher levels. Both "aunts" encourage her to plan and to plan realistically.

While Barbara is forced to hew rather closely to the rigorous standards of her household in terms of cleanliness, dress, and dating behavior, she is treated permissively with regard to her household activities and purchasing behavior. She has never worked at any job for pay even around the house and has no particular tasks around the house assigned to her. On occasion she has taken on something like cleaning out the garage without being asked and has received money in gratitude. But such activities are unusual.

She was given an allowance when she first entered school. With it she purchased the usual candy and soft drinks. The first purchase she can really recall occurred when she was in the third grade. On Mother's Day she slipped away from the house and walked four blocks to the nearest drug store, a trip for which she normally had to ask permission. With one dollar which she had saved from her allowance she bought two small, glass vases —one blue, one pink. She wrapped the vases in newspaper and found a red ribbon with which to tie the package. "It looked sort of cute," she says, "with the black and white of the newspaper. I was really proud of it because I had bought it myself and it wasn't between those two. And, I think they both felt a little better about it, because I had actually saved it myself."

Previously, on all occasions when gifts were appropriate, one or both of the "aunts" would simply select a present and write Barbara's name on as the giver. Perhaps Barbara overstates the saving involved for her first independent gift. At that time she received a weekly allowance of one dollar.

Barbara's present allowance is ten dollars a week. With it she must purchase her cosmetics. But all other normal expenses for items such as school supplies, clothing, and the like are paid for by her "aunts."

Although the purchase to be discussed here is one of a dress for a homecoming dance, it may be useful to examine the way in which Barbara used her allowance during that same week. At the time she was saving money for Christmas. She has a large piggy bank in her room in which she puts small amounts, and she has a savings account. One of her aunts makes deposits in the account for her when Barbara wants to put some of her money in it. None the less, during the week in question Barbara spent eight of the ten dollars.

There were two major expenditures. The first of these was a class pin for the birthday of a white girl friend in her history class. The girl's family had told her that a class ring or any class jewelry would have to come out of her allowance, and she had not purchased anything for that reason. Several weeks earlier she had admired Barbara's pin showing the year of their expected graduation and the name of the school they attend. The pin cost $3. As Barbara says, "She's a very good friend of mine, and she is in my American history class, and I am the only Negro in that class. We just get along fine."

Three more dollars went to the Baptist Church. Barbara normally contributes twenty-five cents a week, but during loyalty month each member is supposed to double his contribution and to designate the organization within the church that is to be credited with the contribution. Barbara is quite active in her church. (She is president of the Youth Choir, secretary of YWA, a member of the Youth Council, and assistant secretary of the Intermediate Sunday School.) Rather than simply doubling her contribution she gave $1 for her regular contribution and $1 each for the Youth Choir and the Intermediate Department.

Of the remaining $4, two went into the piggy bank and $2 went for incidentals: "a hamburger and stuff like that."

Barbara may seem all-of-a-piece, imbued by two of the dominant values of the protestant ethic, propriety and service. But, as in the case of most teenagers, her ambivalences are as characteristic of her as are her consistencies. When asked whom she would most like to be, she replies, "Well, I think I would want to be a little girl that was the only child and that there was both a mother and a father, and very wealthy. I think that's who I would like to be if I wasn't me." The *little* girl she refers to is sixteen years old, just one year younger than Barbara—or, perhaps the age she still thinks herself to be, since she turned seventeen quite recently. Yet, while she wants the protection and affection such a family could give her, she strongly desires the freedom and independence of being an adult.

"I have always seen myself as a career girl, coming home to my apartment with nobody in it but me. And going out when I want to, and no one to say you can't go."

Her ambivalence toward her "aunts" is equally clear and is bound up partially in her concept of fair play and reciprocity. As she says, "Some of the things they want me to do I do just because they asked me to. Then, when I want to do something, they'll say I can't or they'll give some reason why I can't. And sometimes I really and truly want to do it. And it sort of hurts me at times.

"My real aunt, she's more set in her ways than Caroline is. She's the boss, sort of. She has reasons for everything. I mean she'll think of something that I haven't done or something that she told me to do or something I did last year that I wasn't supposed to. Anything, you know. I just sit down and cry sometimes. If I cry loud enough, she'll finally say I can go. Well—sometimes I just stay at home—I thought I was going to have to do it for Homecoming. I asked her on Sunday and she wouldn't tell me all week."

Barbara has developed the personal manners of her society well. She smiles easily and openly. But she can turn sincerely serious the moment such a reaction is appropriate; but it would be an error to think of her as being responsively other-directed in any simple sense. She has a strongly developed concept of her own individuality and is quick to reject any notion that disparages it. In fact, she sees the world as one in which she can control her future within reasonable limits.

She says, "I have always thought, if I didn't become a doctor, I was going to be an interior decorator; and, if I didn't become an interior decorator, I was going to be an airline stewardess; and, if I didn't become an airline stewardess, I would be a physical education teacher. Now I want to be a teacher, and I believe I will stay there. But, if I don't, I can always go back to one of those others."

Barbara is not as self-confident as her easy manner suggests. She is somewhat sensitive about her physical appearance. Of medium height and medium attractiveness, she has a tendency to put on weight, particularly on hip and thigh. She has promised herself several times to take off eight or ten pounds but has had no success. Without being fat, she is, none the less, solid and mildly steatopygous. She describes herself as having looked like a hippopotamus in comparison with the three other girls who were twirlers with her in junior high school.

Further, she has real difficulty in imagining herself as a married woman. Whether this is related to a belief that she will not seem attractive enough to the right sort of boy, fear of losing a social position and the personal freedom that she feels to be within her grasp, or unfamiliarity with the roles and requirements of family life is difficult to say. Her "aunts" mention marriage to her in favorable terms despite their spinsterhood—especially when suggesting that she dress more carefully or take off weight.

Barbara remains unconvinced, unsure, and unready. She wants her own little apartment, at least for a while.

On Sunday James Pratt asked her to go with him to the homecoming game and dance. Jim is a sophomore at a nearby college. His sisters, whom Barbara knows, regard him as extremely handsome. Barbara thinks he is "good enough" looking, but not handsome; however, he can only be regarded as something of a prize, being several years older and in college. Barbara accepted the date tentatively and promised to try to get her "aunts'" approval. In spite of the fact that both "aunts" know the boy's family and regard it to be a "good" family, approval came slowly. On Wednesday morning they seemed to have granted tacit approval when they gave Barbara credit cards to four of the better clothing stores in the city. She was instructed to spend no more than $30 on the dress. At the time Barbara had what are described in local, teenage parlance as six "short" formals and eight "long" formals. Neither she nor her "aunts" gave serious thought to the use of one of these dresses, although Caroline mentioned the possibility.

After school Barbara drove to the central shopping district and found a parking place. The location of the parking place was important simply because it determined the order in which she would visit the stores. The store she went to first was one in which she did relatively little of her purchasing. It was a grey, rainy day. And, since she was immediately in front of store *A*, Barbara shopped there first.

She had several of the dress requirements in mind. She wanted a maroon dress and one with a pleated or flared skirt. The straight lines of many dresses do not flatter Barbara's figure, and she believes that they look "old."

The saleslady in store *A* showed her all of the dresses in her size, being particularly enthusiastic about a red dress. Barbara does not believe that red is a good color for her. (Her favorite color is blue, but she did not consider blue dresses since she has one in blue.) Finally she tried on two dresses, one a plain white, the other maroon. She tried on the white dress first, because it was within her price range. She felt that the dress made her look heavier than she is; and its plainness seemed to her to require either very dramatic looks and coloring or a gloomy personality. Barbara says, "I always look to see whether a dress adds anything to my character or takes away anything." The white dress added nothing and, according to Barbara, made her look darker as well as fatter.

The maroon dress that she tried on made her look lighter in color and slimmer. But it was a bit too decolleté and over the price ceiling that she had been given. If the dress had been perfect for her, she might have called her aunt and explained the situation in hopes of getting approval.

As Barbara says of her aunt, "She likes clothes, period. She has a whole gang of clothes. Everything she has really looks good on her, and she likes to dress. She buys expensive clothes and they last a long while. But she won't let me wear anything of hers and fusses when I even lend a girl friend a sweater." There was good reason to believe that approval for a more expensive dress would be forthcoming, if Barbara could justify it.

While in the store Barbara noticed a blue and white dress that appealed to her. She thought it wrong for the occasion but filed it in her memory as something she might buy a few weeks later.

The second store she visited was store G, next door to store A. Store G has less of an assortment of young dresses than any of the other three. Barbara looked through them briefly but tried none on. Several struck her as being the kind of thing her aunt wore (Barbara's aunt is approximately fifty years old) and inappropriate for a high school girl.

To reach store M, Barbara had to cross one street only. She had told one of the girls in her mathematics class who works in store M to look for a dress for her, particularly for a suitable maroon dress. This was in spite of the fact that she had no credit card for the store. When Barbara arrived her friend, Patsy, said, "Barbara, I cannot find a thing." The two of them talked for awhile about possibilities.

Patsy said, "It's really sort of casual."

Barbara replied, "Yes, but casual-dressy."

Patsy suggested that Barbara could wear a white dress she had with a maroon blazer. Barbara had thought of this earlier but had discarded the combination as not being dressy enough, and her friends had already seen both the dress and the blazer. They suggested several other changes she could work on existing items in her wardrobe, but Barbara took none of them seriously. (It is interesting that Barbara never mentions the fact that maroon and white are the high school colors. Yet, obviously this and the fact that she has no dress of that color are at least partially responsible for the preference on this occasion.)

Having given up on the homecoming dress, Barbara and Patsy looked at several skirt and sweater combinations. As Barbara says, "I like clothes! I really like clothes! And if I see something that I like while I'm looking for something else, I go home and say, 'I saw the cutest little dress or whatever-it-is today. And she'll say, 'Oh, did you?' And most of the time, if I tell her where it was and what color it was and describe it, I eventually end up with it."

Store Q was the fourth store Barbara visited. It is also the store at which she buys most of her clothing. The saleslady there was another friend, this time a colored girl from the local college who ran up and greeted Barbara calling her "Bobbie."

All her friend could find were knitted dresses, which Barbara thinks unsuitable for her figure and refers to as "college-type" dresses. "College-type" clothes are those worn daily by coeds at the local college. Then they looked at maroon skirt and sweater combinations, partly because the skirts were on sale. Since they had run out of possibilities, her friend asked Barbara whether she needed anything else, and Barbara remembered that she was low on bath oil. She purchased that and an after-bath lotion. She charged both, since they do not come under the more restrictive category of cosmetics for which she pays out of her allowance.

At store *J* Barbara walked to the dresses and began to look them over before any salesperson spoke to her. By the time the salesgirl had arrived Barbara had already located a maroon and white dress and was in her words "mooning over it." She looked at several others after locating the maroon and white, but when the salesgirl asked whether she would like to try some on, she took only the maroon and white to the dressing room.

According to Barbara, as soon as she had the dress on she knew it was right. Barbara says, "When I put it on it really looked like me. I mean, it was my character. It fit me, and if I was to take it off and hang it up somewhere, you would walk in and say, 'Oh, that's Bobbie's dress.'"

She did not simply stop at that however. "When I buy things like that without them, I usually ask myself how she (her aunt) will like it. I look at it from all angles and try to see what she would criticize. But I couldn't find any criticisms for *that* dress. I thought she would like it."

According to Barbara it took her less than twenty minutes to get the dress after she entered store *J*. While not a record, this is much less time than she usually takes in selecting a dress. The entire shopping trip took just over two hours from the time she parked her car to the time she walked out of the store with her dress.

When Barbara arrived home her aunt asked what she had bought. Barbara answered, "I bought a stupid dress." Her aunt said, "If it's a stupid dress, why did you buy it?" Barbara said she bought the dress because she liked it. Her aunt said, "That's just like you." Barbara took out the dress and held it up.

Her aunt said, "Hmmmm."

Referring to both "aunts" Barbara says, "When they don't say anything, I know they like it. When they have a criticism, they say it. But, other than that, they won't say anything."

Barbara went into her room and tried on the dress, then returned to the hall where there is a full-length mirror. Caroline arrived at about that time.

"Oh," Caroline said, "this is what you bought."

"Yeah," said Barbara.

"You could have worn that white dress you already have."

Barbara said, "I don't want to wear it."

Caroline said, "You never want to wear what you have."

Barbara's aunt walked into the hall and remarked that Barbara never wanted to wear anything one of them bought her. The discussion was normal for such an occasion, and, if the tone was more than commonplace family banter, Barbara did not realize it. She was, in fact, quite pleased that neither of her "aunts" had developed a specific criticism.

Barbara's aunt noticed the other bag and opened it to see what it contained. "What's this?" she asked.

Barbara said, "I have only a very little bath oil left."

Her aunt said, "That's good, I was about to get some myself." And with that she took the bath oil into her own bathroom. Barbara doubts that she will actually use it, because they prefer different scents. Barbara purchased a bath oil with a distinct lemon odor, an odor she has liked after having had a third grade teacher who smelled "lemony." Barbara's aunt prefers a muskier or more floral scent in bath oils. However, the three women frequently borrow each other's bath oil. It is one of the few things they share.

At 6:30 P.M. on the night of the dance Jim called up to find out whether the date was still "on." Barbara, who had already finished her bath and who was stalling because she dislikes dressing until the last minute, told him she thought it was and asked him to come over at seven.

After the call she dressed and worked on her hair. She went out into the hall to see whether her slip was showing. Caroline asked to look at her, having her turn around. She asked whether Barbara's aunt had pressed the dress, which she thought looked slightly wrinkled. Barbara replied that no one had pressed the dress. Caroline insisted that she take the dress off for a proper pressing and got out the steam iron. After giving it a pressing, she had Barbara put it on again and made a second inspection. "That looks better," she said.

Barbara was putting on cologne when Jim arrived only a minute or two late. With her dress she was wearing her class necklace, two rings that she habitually wears, a charm bracelet, and small rhinestone earrings in her pierced ears. Her shoes were white and gold. Her coat was red with a black collar. And she was wearing a new hat that she had bought for the occasion, a black cashmere and fur cap in the Italian style.

Jim listened politely to the lecture and agreed to get Barbara home by 11:45 P.M. As soon as they were out of the house, Barbara gave a sigh of relief that nothing had gone wrong, and Jim remarked on how mature Barbara looked, dressed up. He had seen her quite infrequently and never before on a date. Twice he had visited her home briefly in preparation for the date and had caught her both times in jeans. She answered his remark with, "Well, sweetheart, I don't run around like that all of the time."

It was a quite satisfactory date for Barbara, and it made an impression on her friends. When she and Jim walked to their seats in the stadium a number of Barbara's friends shouted to her and told her she looked cute. Jim behaved extremely well throughout the game. As a college sophomore, he could easily have assumed superiority to a mere high-school game and have estranged Barbara's friends. The other Negro boys in the crowd are especially sensitive to presumed slights and generally do not get along with strangers. Jim made friends with them easily to Barbara's surprise and pleasure.

Barbara and Jim found a common interest in what she refers to as "classical" music, the show tunes from such plays as *West Side Story* and *My Fair Lady*. And they talked about their favorite singers such as Barbra Streisand and Johnny Mathis. Barbara says, "It's not that her name is the same as mine. She spells it different. It's that she sings on a simple basis. I mean it's not out of the ordinary or real loud. It's really simple. I like simple people."

After the game they went to an eating place for a quick bite. A college friend of Barbara's came in with a date and asked, "Gosh, Bobbie, where have you been looking like that?"

"To the game," Barbara said.

"You go to games looking like that?" her friend exclaimed.

"Sure," Barbara said. She was very pleased.

At the dance Barbara marked the dresses of other girls. She had seen most of them before. But two, a maroon shift with white lace and an orange and green scolloped dress received her favorable notice. She was not able to stay at the dance long with her 11:45 curfew.

Barbara says, "I wish I could have another date with him. He's really nice. I mean he makes a girl feel like she is actually a girl. I mean he doesn't try to be sort of advanced or run over you or something. He seems to be able to fit right in with everybody else or whatever situation he is in."

On Sunday morning (homecoming was Friday) Barbara awakened wanting to wear her new dress to church. There were many people who were important to her who would be there. And very few of them had seen the new dress. But she thought that Jim might attend the church and imagined him saying, "Yea, that's what she had on at the homecoming game." With some reluctance she chose another dress. But she promised herself to wear the new maroon and white on the following Sunday with her little black fur and cashmere cap.

Like most people Barbara contends that she buys what she likes in clothes and gives no real thought to whether they will please anyone else.

Yet it is easy to see that the way in which she uses them contradicts her illusion of independence. Certainly she has internalized the general standards of taste of her culture and her friends; however, she has not completely internalized them and must try consciously to look at her purchases through the eyes of her "aunts" in order to check the differences between generations.

The suggestion is that her personality or character, while important in the choice, may not weigh as heavily as the need to define the social role she plays in sartorial terms. In fact, it seems quite likely that rather than simply choosing clothes to express herself, Barbara may be selecting clothes that camouflage certain aspects of her personality just as she selects a skirt to camouflage the heaviness of her hips. The proclamation of her clothing may not be the bold, "Look, world, this is who I am!" but the more tentative "Please, this is how I want to be considered."

Of course, Barbara is at an age at which she is still trying to discover herself. In effect this process may be largely one of attempting to learn the ways in which the world will consider and accept her. Her experience as a high school student will undoubtedly prove to be useful in the changing consumption patterns that will be appropriate for college, and those, in turn, will provide a background for the ones she will find necessary as a teacher. Whether her personality will undergo much change, it is clear that her preferences in clothing must if she is to work her way through these subsequent roles. And, if she does marry someone like Jim, she will probably dress differently than she would as a single teacher of physical education, not because the unique individual, Barbara Fleming has changed, but because her social role has. None of this suggests that her unique personality does not function in the selection of clothing or will not so function whatever her social role.

A TIME
for PROPOSITIONS

As one considers Juan's shirt, Peter Rigby's furniture, the peach-faced parrot, or Barbara's new dress, there is an enormous temptation to describe consumer behavior in terms of a decision model suggested by economic theory, decision theory, and some portions of psychological theory. This might be stated as:

$$D_a \equiv \frac{AR_a}{AE_a} \geqslant \frac{AR_x}{AE_x}$$

This reads simply decision A will be made, if, and only if, the anticipated reward for the decision divided by the anticipated effort required by the action is at least as great as the anticipated reward of any other decision, divided by the anticipated effort required by that action.[1]

There are a number of problems involved in starting a theory at such a point. First, it suggests that the subject under consideration relates to purchases that are made and need consider little or nothing subsequent to that event. Second, it seems to be an assumption itself and to rest on certain other assumptions that are highly questionable, such as the ability of the human mind to carry out rather difficult mathematical procedures such as the ascription of some sort of reward units to varying situations and effort units to different forms of effort, to say nothing of carrying out a fairly

---

[1] There are, of course, alternative formulations. The most obvious using the same notation is: $D_a \equiv AR_a - AE_a \bigvee AR_x - AE_x$, but minor changes could incorporate the notion of variable reward outcomes, each associated with some predicted probability or other such relative subtleties.

large number of long division problems subconsciously.[2] Further it suggests that what we should be engaged in is a study of human anticipations and evaluation, neither of which is readily accessible to study.

In all probability the implicit assumption that such a model should be the basis for a study of consumer behavior has had more than a little to do with current distortions common to discussions of human behavior. Any beginning effort, should, it would seem, start with a simple listing of the factors, or elements or processes that seem relevant, taking considerable care not to imply relationships for which there is little supporting evidence. I would like to assert two propositions.

> Proposition 1. *Someone goes through some process and acquires something with some effect.*
> Proposition 2. *Someone uses something in some way with some effect.*

I believe that the important character of these propositions lies in what is *not* said, as much as in what is said. The elements of the first proposition are the individual, the product or service acquired, the process that includes acquisition, and the effect. Notice that the proposition does not suggest that the process is directed toward acquisition, but merely includes it. Nor is there any suggestion of what causes the effect or what is effected. Proposition 2 is similarly stripped of many possible implications. The term "uses" is meant in a reasonably broad sense.

Let it be clear that both propositions are required to cover any instance of consumer behavior and that both the *someone* and the *something* remain constant for an individual instance of consumer behavior. An example may help. Imagine a woman purchasing a box of corn flakes that she herself does not eat. We should consider first the "someone." The woman must be characterized by some definitional system unless one wishes to characterize her simply in terms of her behavior in the consumer situation. It would not be irrelevant to describe her in terms of her age, her anxieties or her social class if one were concerned with the possible relationship between these and any other element contained in the propositions. The process that includes purchase could well include putting on a coat, getting out car keys and all the other activities included in going to the store, selecting the product, paying for it, and returning home. The "something" must also be defined in relevant terms. For instance, one might include the grocery bag and savings stamps in the "something" which would then mean that throwing the bag away or folding it up and putting it in a

---

[2] "In part this may be attributed to the realization that game theory is inadequate as a descriptive theory; human beings simply do not have the perception, the memory, or the logical facility assumed by any of the theories," R. Duncan Luce and Howard Raiffa, *Games and Decisions.* New York: Wiley, 1957, p. 259.

drawer and that licking the stamps, and so forth, would have to be included in the use. The effect could include effects on the someone, the something, the process, or any other element of the situation. In fact, the assumption could well be made that there are effects on all elements included in the proposition and quite probably on other elements of the total situation such as the store or the automobile tires or the cashier.

The conclusion is that if any three elements of Proposition 1 are defined, the fourth is also defined. And the adequacy of the definition of the fourth element is a function of the adequacy of the independent definitions of the other three elements. A box of corn flakes is completely defined by the individual who purchases it, the processes involved in the purchase, and the various effects consequent in this behavioral package. For instance, on a fairly trivial level, the box of corn flakes is partially defined by the change in inventory of the store.

The portion of the behavior included in Proposition 2 for the same case includes both the woman and the corn flakes. Her use of the product may consist largely of placing it on a shelf and at some later time throwing the empty box away. (This suggests that the husband or children acquire the corn flakes from the shelf and use them in some way.) Again, a definition of the effects involved in this portion of consumer behavior, combined with definitions of the "someone" and the "something," defines the use. And any one element of the second proposition can be defined in terms of the other three.

The two propositions are, of course, simultaneous propositions. This means that an adequate definition of the someone and the something must satisfy both propositions. There is nothing at all novel in the notion. Its primary value lies in suggesting the range and direction of research required for the development of a theory of consumer behavior.

It should be obvious to any student of the subject that some elements of the propositions have been studied with considerable ingenuity and care by marketing specialists while others have received little attention. Further, some disciplines have tended to develop relatively powerful methodologies that apply to one or two elements or to interrelation between specific elements that are not commonly known or utilized by students of consumer behavior. Lastly, it is obvious that very few attempts have been made to tie all of the elements together into any systematic construct.

In my opinion there is not enough reliable information available for the construction of an operational theory. While models that have aesthetic or intellectual appeal are among the delights of a computer-mathematics age, they can, when misunderstood, delay progress toward viable theory through their almost sirenlike attraction.

The closest thing to a theory of consumer behavior that exists currently is probably some decision model somewhat like that stated at the beginning of this chapter. The elements normally included in one way or another are the cost or effort involved in various actions, the relative rewards anticipated, and the perceived probability that such rewards will in fact follow. Without going into the mathematics of decision making, I would like to suggest why decision theory should be regarded as wrong-headed for the prediction of individual decisions. (I believe that it is, at its present stage of development, also inadequate as a standard for the evaluation of institutional decisions, but the basis for that belief requires a rather involved explanation that is not appropriate here.)

It is common knowledge that human-choice experiments show that people in general do not maximize their chances for reward in any usual sense, but this is often overlooked since it is intuitively obvious that they should.[3] Two of my own recent experiments seem relevant.

In the first, women were offered their choice of any one of four loaves of bread, each marked with a different symbol.[4] Twice-a-week deliveries were made to each woman's door and each made at least twelve repeated selections. In spite of the fact that all loaves of bread were as close to identical as modern, quality-control methods could assure, half of the women developed a marked brand loyalty to one of the symbols. And this brand loyalty was not easily upset by premiums (in the form of coins) placed on other brands. Further, most women tried all or several of the brands prior to demonstrating brand loyalty. There are, of course, numerous explanations for such behavior. Most of them deal with the difference between anticipated reward and objectively measured reward in one way or another. The individual cases of two of the subjects suggests some of the difficulties involved. Subject 1 chose brand P on the first trial and every subsequent trial despite premiums ranging from one to seven cents placed on another loaf. Subject 2 chose brand M on her first trial and alternated her choice each time so that no one of the four brands was ever selected on either of the two trials following its last selection. The first subject's actions can be explained in terms of habit strength, which may be conceived as increased reward anticipation or decreased effort. The second subject's behavior seems to deny either of these explanations. First, the willingness to select any loaf seems to suggest that the anticipated reward for any loaf was identical. If this were true, why should she go to the trouble of remembering which loaf she chose last time in order to avoid it on the next trial? Does one have to

[3] R. R. Bush and F. Mosteller, *Stochastic Models for Learning.* New York: Wiley, 1955, pp. 294-300.
[4] W. T. Tucker, "The Development of Brand Loyalty," *Journal of Marketing Research,* 1, August 1964, pp. 32-35.

refer to the anticipated rewards of novelty where novelty is in fact mini-
mized? Or should one suggest that the subject is continually exploring
to determine what the characteristics of the different brands are? Whatever one suggests, decision theory in the process seems to lose applica-
bility to consumer behavior.

The second experiment attempts to test the relationship of reward, the
probability of reward and effort in the most direct fashion.[5] The apparatus
used is a rather large box with three lifting handles. The subject is given
essentially the following instructions: Your task during the next hour is to
produce 120 buzzes using this apparatus. Select any of the handles you wish
and raise it; if it is the correct handle, a buzzer will sound. If the buzzer
sounds, stop until the machine is reset for you to make another buzz. If the
buzzer does not sound, select either of the two remaining handles. If it causes
the buzzer to sound, wait for the apparatus to be reset. If it does not cause
the buzzer to sound, raise the third handle, which will cause the buzzer to
sound, and wait for the instructions to begin to produce the next buzz.

Since each of the handles is equally likely to be "correct" on any trial,
and since the handles weigh 10, 20, and 30 pounds respectively, it
would seem sensible to lift the lightest handle first, the next lightest second
and the heaviest last on all trials. Subjects (college males) have shown
no inclination to use that solution even when they grow tired and ask
to rest. On the average, subjects have made no apparent attempt to
minimize the total work required, even when given as many as 240 trials
at a single session. We have a saying in our culture, "work is its own
reward." There are other possible explanations involving the gambler's
fallacy, the nature of the social situation, or the desire to show off one's
muscularity. But, if such things influence a situation as simple as the production of buzzes on an apparatus of this sort, one might conclude that
something is always operating in complex consumer behavior to con-
found decision-theory analysis.

It is exactly in order to prevent unwarranted reliance on algebraic
models as essentially accurate explanations for behavior without empirical
evidence that the two propositions suggested here are kept almost unbear-
ably general. They do imply an element of certainty that many would not
posit in relationship to any human behavior. The statement that any
element in either proposition is fully defined by the other three elements
is quite possibly untenable. Certainly a number of theorists would prefer

---

[5] W. T. Tucker, "Human Choice Behavior: The Relationship Between Effort and Probability of Reward," *Marketing and Economic Development:* Proceedings of the American
Marketing Association 1965 Fall Conference; Chicago, American Marketing Association,
1965, pp. 411-418 reports a subsequent experiment that supports the same conclusions.

to say that any element in either proposition is *probabilistically* defined by the other three elements. The restriction is surely legitimate, given the concepts and measuring instruments with which we have to deal.

One other seeming rigidity of the paradigm is its insistence that the someone and something of both propositions are identical. If there are effects included in the matter covered by Proposition 1, is it not likely that either the someone or the something may be effected and therefore become different from the someone or the something that operate in Proposition 1 before the subsequent time period covered by Proposition 2? Much as I dislike admitting this difficulty, there seems no way around it. Some change, even critical change, could occur between the purchase act and the use act. It would be hard to claim that the man who buys an engagement ring is identical with the one who breaks the engagement and returns it. The analogy with simultaneous equations is overstated, but I do not believe that it is a useless analogy.

The propositions are simply organizing and suggestive schemes or perhaps formats. It might be of interest to examine their elements and possible relations in terms of present knowledge and methodology.

Someone

The "someone" element, like the others, craves definition. The number of possible concepts and measuring instruments that can be applied to the task of definition is unbelievably large. With increasing evidence that such things as memory and intelligence have a biochemical base, a whole new range of potential measurement seems to lie just over the horizon. At present most of the paraphernalia of sociology and psychology apply, and the problem is to determine their relevance. Marketing has done most with socioeconomic variables, including geographic location, setting up descriptions or definitions that relate people to product acquisition or use in terms of markets. The enormous amount or work of this sort that has been carried out is of theoretical as well as practical value in that it has developed a resonably broad perspective of the definitional systems applicable to the someone. Age, sex, life-cycle stage, subculture, and socioeconomic variables are clearly relevant. Work on the relevance of psychological variables has been less persuasive with studies by Westfall, Evans, and myself suggesting that we have been trying to examine appropriate variables without adequate measuring instruments or conceptual frames.[6]

[6] F. B. Evans, "Psychological and Objective Factors in The Prediction of Brand Choice: Ford Versus Chevrolet," *The Journal of Business*, 32, October, 1959, pp. 340-369.

Ralph Westfall, "Psychological Factors in Predicting Product Choice," *Journal of Marketing*, 26, April 1962, pp. 34-41.

W. T. Tucker and J. J. Painter, "Personality and Product Use," *Journal of Applied Psychology*, 45, 1961, pp. 325-329.

The oft-mentioned study by Mason Haire of instant coffee nonusers clearly implies that cognitions, attitudes, beliefs, and opinions form a range of constructs with which students of the subject should attempt to deal meaningfully.[7] No study has so clearly verified this as Al E. Birdwell's examination of the relationship between self-image and product image.[8]

There has long been an implicit concept that consumers can be defined in terms of either the products they acquire or use or in terms of the meanings products have for them or their attitudes toward products. Montrose S. Sommers' study is, perhaps, as explicit on this as any recent work.[9] Both he and Bob S. Hodges are currently engaged in research that should suggest how valid and useful definitional systems of this sort may be.

The Process That Includes Acquisition

The cases included in this book are highly persuasive that the process of acquisition is a much more extensive and richer process than we usually think. Juan's shirt, Paul's peach-faced parrot, or Mrs. Superscript's second-hand Cadillac seem deeply imbedded in some total-life process. To speak of the process as though it included only those actions directed toward acquisition is to misunderstand the character of consumer behavior. And to speak of the process only in terms of intentions or instrumental actions may be one of the more ridiculous conclusions of a *post hoc* sort. Attending to a Ford commercial is almost surely a significant portion of the process that includes, or passes through, the acquisition and use of a Chevrolet. It might as easily be a portion of the process that includes the purchase of a camera or the eating of an avocado. The conceptual dangers seem to be of two sorts. First there is the danger of reducing all present behavior to a function of some common past event such as toilet training. The second is the danger of excluding from the study of present behavior those portions of the process that do not seem to be instrumentally or causally linked to it, but which are nonetheless critical to an understanding of the process.

There is no intention here to deny the existence of cause-effect relationships in consumer behavior. The suggestion is simply that other sorts of relationships may be more common, more available to research or more critical to an understanding of the process.

---

[7] Maison Haire, "Projective Techniques in Marketing Research," *Journal of Marketing*, 14, April 1950, p. 649.

[8] Al E. Birdwell, Jr., *A Study of the Influence of Image Congruence on Consumer Choice*, Unpublished Doctoral Dissertation, University of Texas. (A summary is to appear in Proceedings American Marketing Association Conference Dec. 1964.)

[9] Montrose S. Sommers, "The Use of Product Symbolism to Differentiate Social Strata," *University of Houston Business Review*, 11, Fall 1964, pp. 1-102.

Whatever the process is, it should not be considered simply a set of physical actions, although this subset may be one that can be approached most readily. Cognitive processes and interactions are surely as relevant to the process as cognitions are to the definition of consumers. It seems almost redundant to mention that social dynamics may describe portions of the process with greater accuracy than any other conceptual frames. Communications theory and all of the work on audience measurement generally impinge upon the process.

It is necessary to admit the artificiality of a distinction between the individual and what he does. Analysis always seems to sever the most important connective tissue. The legitimizing assumption about the relationship of the elements of both proposition is that any one is defined by an adequate definition of the other three. In effect, this demands the kinds of definitions that will bind the wounds of analysis. In effect, the process must be defined in terms of the someone if it is to satisfy the demands of the propositional form. Of course, it is further assumed that none of the elements can be defined out of situational context.

Reference to Margaret Mead's recent work in Indonesia may suggest the conceptual requirements without implying that hers is the only adequate methodology or even the preferred one. Not only does her work describing the activities of the people being studied include full accounts of behavioral sequences, the individuals involved, and the circumstances under which they occurred; her research team took thousands of feet of film to preserve the connectedness that even the most thorough verbal description loses.[10]

Something

The thing acquired has been variously categorized according to its class, brand, the nature of the one who acquired it, or the presumed character of the acquisition process, narrowly defined. Classification systems that divide goods into large subgroups such as durables and nondurables have uses and should not be derided for their simplicity. Nor should the customary categories such as furniture, hardware, foods, or clothing be disregarded for their obviousness. While neither system satisfies the conditions of clarity and completeness required of a nominal scale, either is so much more precise than the more pretentious nonsense of the marketing text that its directness is refreshing.

More complex systems such as the categories described in terms of presumed acquisition behavior (convenience, shopping, specialty and im-

---

[10] Margaret Mead, "Retrospects and Prospects," *Anthropology and Human Behavior.* Washington, D.C.; The Anthropological Association of Washington, 1963.

pulse) or the newer continua (red-yellow) essay considerably more than they can handle. And such casually used adjectives as "fashion" or "unwanted" should hardly be tolerated by students of the subject. There may even be doubt that marketing practitioners find them of real use except for the convenience of disregarding the fashion or unwanted aspects of certain products.

A study by Keith Cox showing the different effect on sales of different display widths for different products suggests that some existing product definitional systems may be largely unoperational![11]

Of course, there has been almost no help from the behavioral sciences in the definition of contemporary artifacts. The result is that rather than having product definitional systems that can be utilized in the process of understanding the other elements mentioned in the propositions, it seems necessary to use the definitional systems that deal with individuals or processes in the examination of products. Since the definitional systems for individuals is probably the most extensive and possibly valid, it seems probable that our best methods for product description lie in the nature of purchasers and users and in terms of the meanings various sorts of people associate with products. For instance, we might take social class as a variable and discuss the question of whether a specific product is purchased more frequently by one class than another, used more frequently by one class than another, or takes different forms in one class than another.

The statement that 98 percent of the homes in the United States have television sets suggests that one is considering an essentially classless product. And we may assume that the sets are somehow the same since we refer to them all in the same way. But they may be quite different in nature (age, size, original cost, and such other obvious characteristics), in use, or in the meaning assigned them by their owners or users. All of this merely indicates that we are too sophisticated to classify goods in the simplest physical terms such as size or compositions and have no other useful labels or relevant continua for more appropriate definition.

The availability of the computer and the range of techniques suggested by multivariate analysis makes it clear that we can at least proceed to define products in terms of their similarity to other products in a fairly systematic manner. While some current work germaine to the problem is underway, I know of no efforts being made to tackle the question of product similarity directly.

While no mention has been made of services, it should be clear that these are acquired also. In fact, what is most often acquired is some combination or package of services and products more difficult to describe

---

[11] Keith Cox, "The Responsiveness of Food Sales to Shelf Space Changes in Supermarkets," *Journal of Marketing Research,* May 1964, pp. 63-67.

than either alone. Nor is anyone sure where products leave off and services begin. It is not difficult to foresee enormous problems arising out of inadequate attempts to separate products and services or failures to take the service aura of particular products into account. At the simplest level, the presence of a guarantee may differentiate otherwise similar products.

The additional consideration of service is conceptually negligible in the total scheme of consumer behavior. It does, however, pose research considerations of no mean measure. There are no ready simplifications; only the *caveat*.

Effects

Effects *within* the system are at once the most difficult and the simplest to discuss. What can be affected? Only those things discussed as other elements. How can they be affected? Only in the terms in which they are defined.

These statements are not as trivial as they may at first appear. The cases in this volume are rather fully described, but in few of them is there more than slight opportunity to understand effects within the system. For instance, the processes involved in the Rigbys' purchase of furniture for their sons almost certainly were accompanied by cognitive changes about furniture, furniture retailers, the merchants of their own town, and a host of other things. It is not difficult to imagine what some of these were since the article itself is suggestive of their nature. But such suggestions are a far cry from measurement and satisfactory quantification of effect.

The case discussed by Pullins ends with a statement, "*At this time,* the values that Bob has placed on Budweiser and Michelob coincide with his conception of his social position." But any changes that may occur through future behavior can be located only if one measures the values with an instrument sensitive enough to examine changes, only if one has a clear definition of "coincidence," only if one can define social position with accuracy and measure Bob's conception of it.

The presence of the effect element in the propositions places major demands on the definitional systems for each of the other elements, demands that might otherwise be unnoticed.

Few attempts have been made to study effects of purchase or use. The most dramatic studies relate to the purchase and use of TV sets and describe behavioral changes in relatively gross ways. Others have studied such limited relationships as that of automobile ownership and academic performance in high-school students. And there have been incidental findings such as the fact that a recent purchaser of a product is one of the most attentive persons to advertisements of the product he has purchased, suggesting that the mere act of purchase may involve particular anxieties, ambivalences, cognitive dissonance or the like. The findings could as easily suggest the individual was merely restimulating certain pleasurable processes or fantasies usually associated with the prepurchase period.

Of course, there are effects that relate to other individuals who may appear in the contextual situations of purchase or use or to other aspects of the physical situation. For instance, if the woman who purchased the corn flakes mentioned earlier purchased the last box on the supermarket shelf, her purchase could influence the behavior of a number of subsequent customers.

There seems to be little reason for going into further examples of the many sorts of effects possible.

All of the elements of Proposition 2 are like the elements in the first proposition. The consumer and the individual are identical (within the suggested limits), use is viewed as imbedded in processes just as acquisition was, and effects of the same kinds are possible; but, while it may be possible to assume identity of the individual and the product from purchase to use in many or most cases, there is the strong presumption that a subsequent instance of purchase may find many of the elements changed by the effects of the previous purchase or use or both. The propositions merely form a system for the segmentation of what is an ongoing process. The product purchased may play an important role in the process of purchasing a subsequent product as the use of an automobile implicates the purchase of gasoline and facilitates the visit to a shopping center. Processes that include the purchase of one item may include the purchase of several. Or the processes involved in the purchase of some item such as a house may span the processes involved in the purchase of a large number of others. And so the segmentation is to some extent arbitrary.

The nature of the suggested elements may tend to minimize the importance of special subportions of the purchase or use activities. A summary of the cases included in this volume would have to emphasize the lack of adequate information apparently available to the purchaser, since most of the examples stress the way in which the consumer searches for relevant knowledge, yet remains incompletely informed at the time of purchase.

An apparent shortcoming of the propositional forms used is that they insist upon both acquisition and use. The case of ToNiri's attempt to buy a house, which seems to be a coherent and complete case of consumer behavior, lacks both, if one considers the time period through the failure of his bid. Great as the temptation may be to include nonacquiring behavior sequences as consumer behavior, even relatively cursory analysis demonstrates the madness involved in attempting to discuss products not purchased. A house was not the only thing ToNiri failed to acquire. The sequence of events reported so ably by Salisbury, insofar as they are a part of some consumer behavior, refer to the purchases of lumber, nails, and other materials with which ToNiri has begun to build.

None of these shortcomings seem vital to the purposes for which the propositions are designed. Their intention is to delimit the subject of consumer behavior clearly, to state where the relevant parameters lie in relation to one another, to suggest the research that could provide satisfactory raw material for a theory, and to provide a set of standards against which any posited theory can be evaluated.

Suggested Readings
in Human Behavior

The materials relevant to human behavior, and therefore applicable to consumer behavior, are voluminous and varied. Certainly no one has made even a start at reading them all. This suggested list contains some of the works with which one might begin to approach the several sub-areas of the subject. Categorizing such work must be arbitrary for the behavioral sciences are less clearly segmented than they seemed two decades ago.

Anthropology and Sociology

Barnouw, Victor, *Culture and Personality*. Homewood, Illinois: Dorsey, 1963.

Bendix, Reinhard, and Seymour Lipset, *Class, Status and Power*. New York: Free Press, 1953.

Benedict, Ruth, *Patterns of Culture*. Boston: Houghton Mifflin, 1934.

Blau, Peter M., *Exchange and Power in Social Life*. New York: Wiley, 1964.

Foster, George M., *Traditional Cultures and the Impact of Technological Change*. New York: Harper and Row, 1962.

Gillin, John, *For a Science of Social Man*. New York: Macmillan, 1954.

Hawley, Amos, *Human Ecology*. New York: Ronald, 1950.

Herskovits, Melville J., *Economic Anthropology*, 2d ed. New York: Knopf, 1952.

Kroeber, Alfred L., ed., *Anthropology Today: An Encyclopedic Inventory*. Berkeley, Calif.: University of California Press, 1953.

Kuhn, Alfred L., ed., *The Study of Society*. Homewood, Illinois: Dorsey, 1963.

Malinowski, Bronislaw, *Magic, Science, Religion and Other Essays*. New York: Free Press, 1948.

Mead, Margaret, *New Lives for Old*. New York: Morrow, 1956.

Nadel, S. F., *The Foundations of Social Anthropology*. Cohen and West, 1951.

Parsons, Talcott, Edward Shils, Kaspar Naegel, and Jesse R. Pitts, ed., *Theories of Society*. New York: Free Press, 1961.

Rogers, Everett M., *Diffusion of Innovations*. New York: Free Press, 1962.

Schram, Wilbur, ed., *Mass Communications,* rev. ed. Urbana, Ill.: University of Illinois Press, 1960.

Sorokin, P. A., *Social and Cultural Dynamics*. Boston: Porter Sargent, 1957.

Weber, Max, *The Theory of Social and Economic Organizations,* trans. by Talcott Parsons. New York: Oxford University Press, 1947.

Economics

Clarkson, Geoffrey P. E., *The Theory of Consumer Demand*. Englewood Cliffs, N.J.: Prentice-Hall, 1963.

Duesenberry, James S., *Income, Saving and the Theory of Consumer Behavior*. Cambridge, Mass.: Harvard University Press, 1949.

Friedman, Milton, *A Theory of the Consumption Function*. Princeton, N.J.: Princeton University Press, 1956.

Henderson, J. M. and R. E. Quandt, *Microeconomic Theory*. New York: McGraw-Hill, 1958.

Hicks, J. R., *A Revision of Demand Theory*. New York: Oxford, 1956.

Marshall, Alfred, *Principles of Economics,* 8th ed. London: Macmillan, 1930.

Papandreou, A. G., *Economics as a Science*. Philadelphia: Lippincott, 1958.

Samuelson, P. A., *Foundations of Economic Analysis,* 5th ed. New York: McGraw-Hill, 1961.

Veblen, Thorstein, *The Theory of the Leisure Class*. New York: Modern Library, 1934.

Marketing

Alderson, Wroe, *Dynamic Marketing Behavior*. Homewood, Illinois: Irwin, 1965.

Bliss, Perry, ed., *Marketing and the Behavioral Sciences*. Boston: Allyn and Bacon, 1963.

Britt, Steuart Henderson, ed. *Consumer Behavior and the Behavioral Sciences*. New York: Wiley, 1966.

Clark, Lincoln H., ed., *Consumer Behavior*. New York: Harper & Row, 1958.

Cox, Reavis, Wroe Alderson, and Stanley J. Shapiro, eds., *Theory in Marketing*. Homewood, Illinois: Irwin, 1964.

Day, Ralph L., ed., *Marketing Models: Quantitative and Behavioral*. Scranton, Pa.: International Textbook, 1964.

Ferber, Robert, and Hugh G. Wales, eds., *Motivation and Market Behavior*. Homewood, Illinois: Irwin, 1958.

Howard, John A., *Marketing: Executive and Buyer Behavior*. New York: Columbia University Press, 1963.

Katona, George, *The Powerful Consumer*. New York: McGraw-Hill, 1960.

McNeal, James U., *Dimensions of Consumer Behavior*. New York: Appleton, 1965.

Martineau, Pierre D., *Motivation in Advertising*. New York: McGraw-Hill, 1957.

Newman, Joseph W., ed., *On Knowing the Consumer*. New York: Wiley, 1966.

Zaltman, Gerald, *Marketing: Contributions from the Behavioral Sciences*. New York: Harcourt, 1965.

Psychology and Social Psychology

Berelson, Bernard and Gary A. Steiner, *Human Behavior: An Inventory of Scientific Findings*. New York: Harcourt, 1965.

Biderman, Albert D., and Herbert Zimmer, eds., *The Manipulation of Human Behavior*. New York: Wiley, 1961.

Brown, Roger, *Social Psychology*. New York: Free Press, 1965.

Cartwright, Dorwin, and Alvin Zander, *Group Dynamics*, 2d ed. New York: Harper & Row, 1960.

Cohen, Arthur R., *Attitude Change and Social Influence*. New York: Basic Books, 1964.

Coleman, James C., *Abnormal Psychology and Modern Life*, 2d ed. Chicago: Scott, Foresman, 1956.

Goffman, Erving, *The Presentation of Self in Everyday Life*. Edinburg: The University of Edinburg Press, 1958.

Hall, Calvin S., and Gardner Lindzey, *Theories of Personality*. New York: Wiley, 1957.

Hilgard and Marquis' Conditioning and Learning, rev. by Gregory A. Kimble. New York: Appleton, 1961.

Kretch, David, Richard S. Crutchfield, and Egerton L. Ballachey, *Social Psychology*. New York: McGraw-Hill, 1962.

Shibutani, Tamotsu, *Society and Personality*. Englewood Cliffs, N.J.: Prentice-Hall, 1961.

Skinner, B. F., *Science and Human Behavior*. New York: Macmillan, 1953.

Southwell, Eugene A., and Michael Merbaum, *Personality: Readings in Theory and Research.* Belmont, California: Wadsworth, 1964.

Vinacke, W. Edgar, Warner R. Wilson, and Gerald M. Meredith, eds., *Dimensions of Social Psychology.* Chicago, Scott, Foresman, 1964.

Wepman, Joseph W., and Ralph W. Heine, *Concepts of Personality.* Chicago: Aldine, 1963.

Woodworth, Robert S., and Harold Schlosberg, *Experimental Psychology.* New York: Holt, Rinehart and Winston, 1962.